Time & the Triplets Three

SAM DEAN

© Sam Dean 2020.

All rights reserved. No part of this work may be reproduced in any form, without written permission from Sam Dean, except in the case of brief quotations.

Publishing in the United Kingdom by Sam Dean

Written by Sam Dean

Graphics created by Olya Milokhina
https://www.behance.net/oleftina_ua/moodboards
Edited by Sian-Elin Flintfreel sianelin.flintfreel@gmail.com
Book design & layout by Velin@Perseus-Design.com

Contact Sam Dean the author samdean@timothybook.shop

ISBN Number:
978-1-80049-032-1 (Paperback)
978-1-80049-031-4 (Ebook)

Visit Timothy's website www.timothybook.shop and download the extra resources including;

- Mr Yeastly's recipes
- Nan's favourite cheese jokes
- Uncle Fingers famous crimes
- Competitions & Quizzes
- Timothy's mum list of nice things to do for friends
- Cousin Lucy's beauty tips
- Father Mike's best top ten hymns
- Timothy's advice if you are being bullied.

Foreword

Thank you for buying this book, I hope it will give you lots of fun and laughter as you discover Timothy's world – his lovely family, great friends, daft and nice teachers, wicked bullies and the amazing journey they all go on together.

I have been bullied and lots of my family and friends have suffered at the hands and mouths of nasty bullies. I felt very lonely and I thought the bullies would ever leave me alone. Thankfully I was able to find a few people who I could trust and with their help I did find a way to move my life forward.

Timothy & the Triplets Three

Have fun reading this book and if you or a friend is struggling to cope with bullies use the resources on my website or use the links at the end of the book to find help and a way forward. You are not alone.

A special thanks to the children who were kind enough to help me review the early draft of this book. My Top-Secret Readers were;

- Maggie
- Finley
- Finn
- Nathan
- Lily
- Joe
- Alex

A big thanks to Sian, Olya and Velin the professionals who make my silliness look like

Timothy & the Triplets Three

a real book. But the biggest thanks goes to my family for their support, patience, energy and love. They know without their help this book could never have been written.

Visit Timothy's website www.timothybook.shop and download the extra resources including;

- Mr Yeastly's recipes
- Nan's favourite cheese jokes
- Uncle Fingers famous crimes
- Competitions & Quizzes
- Timothy's mum list of nice things to do for friends
- Cousin Lucy's beauty tips
- Father Mike's best top ten hymns
- Timothy's advice if you are being bullied.

Sam Dean

Contents

Foreword 3

Cast of Appearance 9

Chapter 1: Timothy... 17

Chapter 2: Money makes the world go around... 29

Chapter 3: The amazing Father Mike rockstar... 39

Chapter 4: Neddy, Eddy and Bert Fullofsnot 47

Chapter 5: Ralph the Debt Collector 57

Chapter 6: Lulabella Queen of America.............. 73

Chapter 7: Dad's surprise birthday cake 85

Chapter 8: Mr Yeastly bakes................................ 97

Chapter 9: Triplets ruin a birthday.....................113

Chapter 10: Jaws 12 Horror Movie.................... 135

Chapter 11: Mad Dog Muncher Triumphs 149

Chapter 12: Living with a Saint 161

Timothy & the Triplets Three

Chapter 13: The Amazing Lulabella 173

Chapter 14: Timothy's Christmas list 181

Chapter 15: Christmas Mashup 187

Chapter 16: Mrs Ritkiks sings 195

Chapter 17: Half a Christmas tree 201

Chapter 18: Grotesque triplet bullies 213

Chapter 19: Fantastic `Around the
World` Advent Calendar 221

Chapter 20: The last day of term 233

Chapter 21: The Growing Christmas Gravy 249

Chapter 22: Turkey Trifle 261

Chapter 23: Crying over cakes 265

Chapter 24: Going to the 50p shop in the sky ... 279

Chapter 25: Mrs Hen 285

Chapter 26: Best Friends 297

Chapter 27: The Fullofsnots visit 311

Chapter 28: Dad makes a donation 319

Chapter 29: The end of CRABz 335

Resources to use if you need help
due to bullying 343

Cast of Appearance

Bert

Cousin Lucy

Crazy Chris
Smasher

Dad

Father Michael

Eddy

Lulabella

Mad Dog Muncher

Mr Fullofsnot

Mr Himalya

Mrs Fullofsnot

Mr Yeastly

Mrs Giswellian

Mrs Hen

Mrs Kingspan

Mrs Whitehead

Mum

Nan

Neddy

Prince Humphey
of Denmark

Stevo

Timothy

Uncle Fingers

Chapter 1
Timothy

When Timothy was 12 years old he lived at 36 Ambrose Close. He was not sure why it was called Ambrose Close; it was not close to anything other than the council garden depot. Why would you want to call a road Ambrose Close-to-a-council-garden-depot? But that is where he lived.

He shared the house with his mum (who was lovely), his dad (who was daft), and Lulabella, his big sister (who told everyone she was amazing). Actually, Lulabella was away at university in

Timothy & the Triplets Three

America; he missed her. Lulabella was Timothy's best big sister. In fact, Lulabella was Timothy's only sister, but still the best.

Most of his life was fun. But, at school, Timothy struggled because of some bullies. The problem was there were three of them, triplets. The triplet bullies were a blight on a life that was otherwise brilliant.

Timothy spent his days helping his lovely mum, laughing at his daft dad's daft jokes and having FaceTime calls with Lulabella when she updated him on how her amazingness had increased since they last spoke.

Timothy had white, fluffy hair, fingernails which he bit most days, and he often had a pre-teen spot on the left-hand side of his nose. It never appeared on the right-hand side of his nose – that was reserved for his five freckles.

Timothy & the Triplets Three

He loved life, but the
bullies in his life made
his life unbearable at
times. They didn't make
every day unbearable,
but they were a constant
and real threat to his
happiness. He didn't
want to walk away, back
down or live in their shadow,
because living in the shadows
was a job for snails and slugs. Timothy
knew he was not a slug or a snail and he
had no intention of becoming one just because
it suited the tiny minds of the bullies.

Timothy was born with white hair. His dad
said it was because it was snowing on the night he
was born. His mum said it was because he was so

Timothy & the Triplets Three

shocked at his dad's driving on the way to hospital to be born. Lulabella said she did not care why he had such white hair, but it did mean that she teased him kindly about his white hair, which was fluffy at the back of his head. So, she nicknamed him Fluffy-do-dah-day, Fluffy-dunk-a-delicious, and Whitefluff–dabby–ditsey-lala-loo. These were just his everyday nicknames from his big sister, but at special times of the year she gave him special versions of his nicknames. At Halloween she called him Fla-pumpkin. At Christmas, she called him Fla-who-dolf and at Easter, in honour of the Easter Rabbit, she called him Fla-Hop. However, the triplet bullies used different words for his hair – ones that were nowhere near as nice.

His family were full of fun and he knew that they loved him. That helped. He also had some

Timothy & the Triplets Three

great friends at school, but they had the same constant threat from the bullies. His friends reacted in different ways when they got the attention of the bullies. Some of his friends only ever looked at their feet when the bullies walked past. Some of them never smiled and grew more and more sad each day. Some bit their nails, or chewed their gums, or just felt sick in their tummies. That was the effect of the triplet bullies.

Timothy learnt that he did not have to commit any great crime to fall foul of their tempers. He could just happen to be in front of the bullies in the dinner queue or sit in front of them in class. Both of these mistakes could lead to chewing gum in his hair, being tripped up in front of his friends, or nasty bruises which needed to be hidden from Mum when he got home.

Timothy & the Triplets Three

He knew he should stand his ground, punch them before they punched him. He knew "sticks and stones may break my bones but names will never hurt me", but actually, their nasty names did hurt him. He tried to turn the other cheek, he tried to stay out of their way, he even tried to become part of the bullying gang at one time, but none of it worked.

There had to be a way out of the bullying misery if he was to be able to relax and enjoy life. If only he could walk home without always looking over his shoulder, if he could stand in a queue without being kicked. He was confident there was a solution out there waiting for him, he just wished it would hurry up and happen.

Sadly, as his school life was marred by miserable bullies who tried to wreck every day, destroy every moment of fun and break his soul, he started to dream of teaching the bullies a lesson they would never forget. Perhaps the lesson would be that he showed them that he, like Lulabella, was amazing too.

He had endured lots of attention from the bullies. They had laughed at him, pushed him, nudged him, stolen his lunch and called him names. The bullies took great pride in mocking him, tripping him up and belittling him in front of the whole class – and that last example was the Teacher Bullies. Oh yes, it was not only the triplets who were bullies in school, some of the teachers were not very nice either.

He was known at school for infuriating teachers by answering questions before they were asked. "Paris", or "1066" or "Bobby Charlton", he would shout out from the front seat in class.

Timothy & the Triplets Three

Timothy was often banned from answering any questions for fear that no other child would ever hear their own voice in the classroom. So, whilst in school lessons, sitting on his hands and listening silently to the rest of his class issue muffled answers of "Barcelona", "1028" and "Lobby Barlton", he would dream of greatness. He would dream of climbing Mount Everest, but he thought it would be too cold. Winning the F1 series would be fun, but he worried it would be too dangerous. Winning the salmon fishing contest on the River Dee could be the answer – hmmm, possibly too wet.

There was another incredible characteristic that Timothy possessed – he had a huge heart. His heart was so full of love and niceness it was really, really big. He tried every day to forgive the bullies, but even though his heart was a big as a galaxy, he did sometimes dream of making them suck giraffe diarrhoea through his dad's sweaty sock.

He had learnt to get home using different routes whenever the bullies said they were going to "get him after school". But that never seemed to work because they always found him. They had encouraged some of his friends not to play with him anymore and hid his clothes under the benches in the changing room after football. However, Timothy knew that he only got his fair share of nastiness from these bullies and that most of his friends suffered in the same way as he did.

This did not stop him dreaming of the day, one day, when he would be able to get his sweet revenge on the members of CRABz (the Chorlton Range Agro Boot Boyz), as the gang of

Timothy & the Triplets Three

bullies was known locally. Timothy wished he lived somewhere, anywhere other than Chorlton Range. Imagine if he lived in Darlington Ridge, then the bullies would have been known as DRABz, or better still, if he lived in Brighton, surely they would be known as BABz. Then the gang might have stayed at home and just picked each other's noses instead.

Timothy was asleep, not snoring like his dad, but fast asleep. I am not quite sure why he would be described as 'fast' asleep, when he was definitely not moving about in his bed. In fact, he rarely moved when he was fast asleep. But fast asleep he was.

It is true to say that Timothy was fast when he wasn't asleep. He was really quick. He was a quick learner and a quick thinker. If there had been a quick-thinking race in the Olympics he would have won the gold medal. If motorways had been made for thinking, Timothy would have been so quick he would be in the outside lane. He would be a jet engine thinker, like a fighter jet thrusting at twice the speed of sound. Timothy would break the sound barrier and startle the crows. Whilst others pondered and wondered, he thought fast and quick. Whilst they deliberated on ham or cheese for sandwiches at lunch, Timothy would order both. But this night, Timothy was 'fast' asleep in bed – not being fast at all.

Timothy was dreaming that one day CRABz would meet their grizzly demise. He just hoped he would be there to see it. His mind was also full of questions:

When would the bullies ever stop?

When would they grow up?

Timothy & the Triplets Three

When would he grow up?

When would a masked superhero fly down and sort out his awful life?

Chapter 2
Money makes the world go around

Each week, Timothy had to give the bullies his pocket money, which meant he never had enough to pay for his lunch. This made him very keen on making money for himself, and he always had lots of business ideas.

Timothy was only five years old when he put a cardboard sign outside his parents' house advertising a 'Garage Sale'. Passers-by were surprised when Timothy answered the front door

Timothy & the Triplets Three

and he tried to sell them the actual garage – it was a simple enough mistake.

He practised his money making by playing games. He was a master of Monopoly – he would win by wearing the other players out. He never took a toilet break and would refuse all food and drink, and stopped his challengers from having any either. Eventually his opponents would tearfully back off and concede defeat by going home and filling up on crisps and fizzy drinks.

One of his projects to raise money was to collect football memorabilia to resell on the internet. He had been quite successful with a football sock from Woolton Wanderers' famous goalie, Lankey Rarms, that he bought for £10 and resold to someone in Kathmandu for £12. (This £2 profit was swallowed by the £25 postal charge, but Timothy's mum never told him about that.) He also traded mud from the football boot of Kuan-wu (a well know Taiwanese forward from Blinky Rovers Northern) for a sweatband from Ronny Silver-Balls, a defender who played for Neverton United. Timothy wasn't sure the mud had come off Kuan-wu's boot, but anyway the boy who bought it had been happy to swap it for the sweatband. He got a tidy profit by selling that sweatband.

To help his research, Timothy bought the *Dragons' Den* box set with the birthday money his sister gave to him. He would watch the nervous entrepreneurs bid to get an investment and then he would recite their sales pitches by heart to amuse Nan. But Nan wasn't amused. However, Nan was not amused at most things. Come to think about it, Timothy had never seen Nan amused at anything, even when Aunty

Timothy & the Triplets Three

Jemima's false teeth fell out of her mouth when she was taking Holy Communion at Mass one Sunday. Everybody else in church laughed about it for weeks, but not Timothy's Nan.

Nan would come to Timothy's house on the bus, which she said was late, dirty and expensive. She would tell Timothy how boring all the soap operas were and why it was a waste of time watching them. Timothy could not understand why she watched them if they were a waste of time but Nan explained that if she didn't watch them she would have nothing to talk about at bingo on Sunday nights.

Timothy & the Triplets Three

Although Nan loved going to the bingo, she said it was fixed so that other people always won the Weekly Super Prize. Nan also said the bingo caller would put chewing gum on the bottom of the bingo balls she needed so that she could never win. When Nan went on one like that, Timothy would look at Dad and they would both roll their eyes in disbelief.

Nan would grumble about the discount shop at the end of her road; it was called the 50p shop.

Timothy loved going to the 50p shop with Nan because he would ask her, "How much is this, Nan?"

"50p," his Nan would bark.

"Oh thanks. How much is this, Nan?" he would ask politely.

"It's 50p, everything is 50p, that's why it's called the 50p shop." His Nan would grind her teeth. (Actually, they weren't her teeth, they belonged to the dentist at the Co-op by the roundabout. She had never paid for them because she said they were awful, but for the purposes of this story we are going to call them Nan's teeth.)

"Oh, ok, thanks Nan," Timothy would say with a saintly smile and a glint in his eye.

His pocket money would be used to buy out-of-date chocolate bars for 1p each (50 of them in a pack = 50p) and sell them at school to unsuspecting bullies for 50p each. Timothy took some pleasure in selling them to the bullies because he could dream at night that they had spent all evening on the loo, rolling around in agony as another out-of-date chocolate bar squiggled out of their bum. The next day, he would sell them more out-of-date chocolate bars at 50p.

If his customer (he liked to use official terms like that because it sounded professional) was a really big bully or very mean to smaller kids, Timothy would always be prepared to do BOGOF deals (Buy one, get one free) in the hope it meant they spent twice as long on the loo that night rolling around in agony. The reality was that the bullies were never able to get off the bog. Some of the bullies who loved chocolate ended up just eating his out-of-date chocolate and living on the bog (never able to BOG-OFF).

He loved helping his customers to get good deals. Timothy thought that there was something poetic about using his business talents to beat the bullies, because they were never bright enough to understand why they were sat on the loo all night, returning the next day to buy more cut price putrid chocolate bars. Being a bully also meant they had to be cool, so they wouldn't tell their mates what had happened, which meant none of them caught on. Once a big bully stole a chocolate bar from Timothy. Instead of making Timothy angry, this made him smile and he slipped an extra free bar into the bully's bag when he wasn't looking. This particular big bully had the next three days off school with squidgy bum.

Sometimes he would cycle past a local bully's house in the evening just to see the light on in the loo, listening to the yowls of agony, and watching the dark green stench waft out of the smallest torture room in the house as the victim parted with yet another out-of-date chocolate bar. He would giggle all the way home.

He wished the bullies would attack him when he was with his miserable, joyless Nan, because he was sure she would make mincemeat out of them. One day, when Timothy was on a bus with his nan, a couple of boys were slightly rude to her. She stood up, pulled the emergency cord, and screamed at them whilst giving them both a huge wedgie, then pulled their baseball caps over their eyes and shoved two raw eggs into their mouths. She then pushed them off the bus. As the bus pulled away, leaving the rude boys in the middle of nowhere, they were both crying. Nan sat back down, rubbed her hands and went back to being silently miserable. It was one of the best days ever.

Chapter 3
The amazing Father Mike rockstar

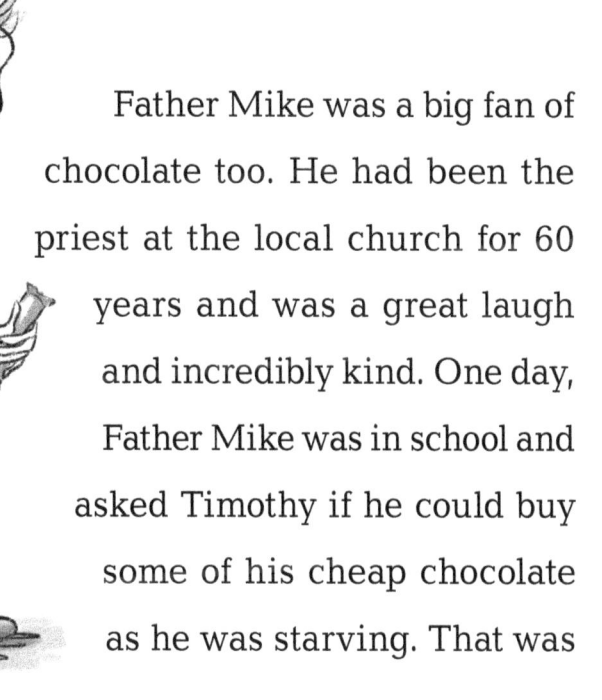

Father Mike was a big fan of chocolate too. He had been the priest at the local church for 60 years and was a great laugh and incredibly kind. One day, Father Mike was in school and asked Timothy if he could buy some of his cheap chocolate as he was starving. That was awkward. Timothy said he was so sorry but he had none left. However, the priest saw a few bars peeking out of his top pocket and insisted on buying them. As a result, Father Mike did not get off the loo for three days and had to conduct the Mass by shouting from the loo in church. He used one toilet roll per service that Sunday.

It was common knowledge that Father Mike had long ago forgotten he was a priest. He believed he was an international singing star, breaking out into 'Who Let The Dogs Out?' during his sermon. He would apologise for having to say prayers and was seen consuming all the holy wine on more than one occasion, before anybody else could even get a sip. At 83, he was the oldest priest in the diocese, but they could not release him, as there was no one left to replace him.

Timothy & the Triplets Three

They had sent young Father Pavel from Gdansk, but his lack of English, heavy black eyebrows, smelly feet and poorly shaven chin had proven too much for the congregation. On balance, they preferred the forgetful, rock singing, but delightful Father Mike. Father Pavel would stand in church with his hands clasped tightly behind his back, rocking on the balls of his feet, whereas Father Mike would do encores for a congregation when they gave him a standing ovation.

The final straw came when young Father Pavel was reluctant to move into Father Mike's flat that was home to his collection of snakes. At the last count, Father Mike had 76 snakes. This was a problem for young Father Pavel, because on the previous count there had been 84 snakes. Father Mike did not have a clue where the other

Timothy & the Triplets Three

8 snakes had gone, but he told Father Pavel not to worry as they would turn up somewhere.

So a petition was started by Timothy's nan, which got over 6,000 signatures, and Father Mike was persuaded to stay on. Young Father Pavel was dispensed back to Gdansk. Apparently, he never arrived. What exactly happened to him was a bit of a mystery. Mrs Squidelia said she'd heard he had joined a rock band in Dover. Mrs Jinel said he had married a farmer's daughter in the South of France. But Timothy's dad speculated his lack of English skills meant he was most probably still trying to navigate the M25.

To be fair to him, Father Mike was amazing when you sat down and thought about it. He had christened Mr and Mrs Arefal's son Elvis instead of Edward. He had married Beyoncé and Stormzy two years ago – which came as quite surprise to

Timothy & the Triplets Three

Jane Smith and Bill Bright, but they went along with it and are happily married to this day.

It was, however, upsetting when he buried John Swinney a few months ago instead of his sister Joan. John was surprised to hear his name read out as he stood by the grave – but even he had to admit it was a lovely eulogy. But thankfully (according to Father Mike), John popped his clogs just a week later so everything was ok in the end. Father Mike even joked at John's funeral that he could have sworn he had already buried him. Maybe this was a bit too soon for the Swinney family, as a silence fell across the congregation, but the organist broke into '7 Rings' by Ariana Grande and all was well.

At the end of a service, Father Mike would always pose for photos and sign autographs. Last Christmas, he circulated locks of his own hair with CD's of his music. Timothy had received Father

Timothy & the Triplets Three

Mike's version of Billie Eilish's 'Bad Guy', whilst his mum was excited to receive Father Mike's remake of 'Sunflower' by Post Malone and Swae Lee.

Timothy's dad thought there was more than age affecting Father Mike's memory. He said his breath often smelt less of wine gums but rather something bought from the local wine shop. But Timothy's mum told his father not to be wicked, she had smelt his breath and it was obviously the Fisherman's Friends Sore Throat Lozenges he used for his chesty cough. Dad laughed and said he agreed the smell might be a Fisherman's Friend, but not the sore throat lozenges.

Timothy & the Triplets Three

Mum's frown made Timothy and Lulabella laugh until there were tears rolling down their cheeks.

Once, in the weeks before Easter, Father Mike had told the congregation they should all give something up for Lent. Mum gave up cream cakes and wine, Lulabella gave up crisps, sugar, cakes, sweets, biscuits, shampoo and (unfortunately) deodorant. Timothy gave up garlic, shellfish and tofu (which was excellent, because he hated all of them). Dad announced he had filled out an Organ Donor Card at work because his boss had made him do it. He thought this would count for Lent because, in the event that he died, he would be giving up his organs. Mum and Lulabella laughed so much their tummies hurt.

"What on earth could you donate?" they asked. "Your eyes are short sighted, your heart is too big, your liver and kidneys have had far too much Prosecco..."

Dad sighed and said, "Well, it's the thought that counts."

Lulabella did not go to church, much but she adored Lent. Sometimes she would give up so many things she had to write the list down in case she forgot what she had given up and ate it by mistake. Timothy had to admit that, for this, she was amazing, because she must hold the unofficial world record of giving things up for Lent. She once suggested to Father Mike that she was going to give up Lent for Lent. Mum had to explain why you can't give Lent up for Lent. Lulabella was disappointed and went into a sulk but soon got over it when Timothy blew a raspberry which made them all laugh.

Chapter 4
Neddy, Eddy and Bert Fullofsnot

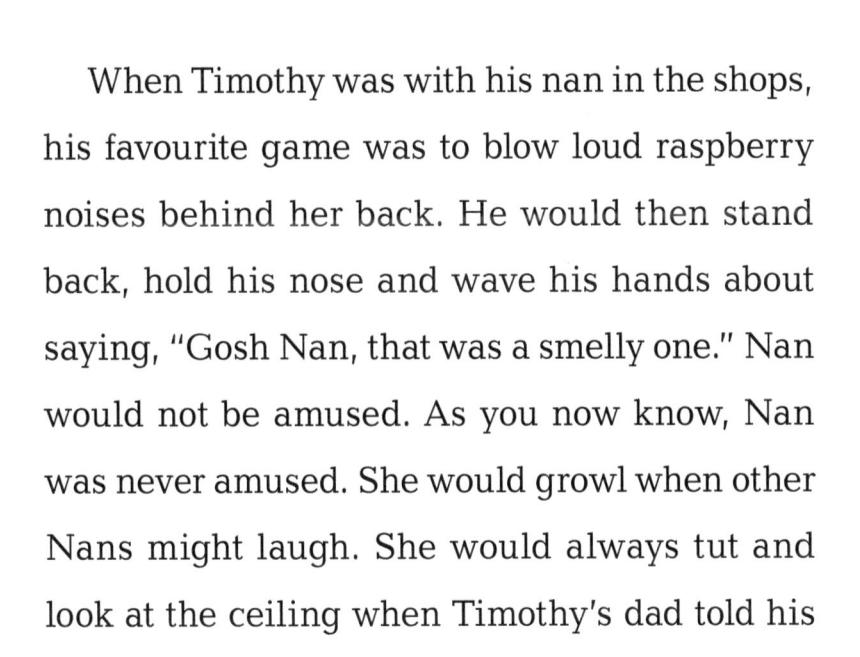

When Timothy was with his nan in the shops, his favourite game was to blow loud raspberry noises behind her back. He would then stand back, hold his nose and wave his hands about saying, "Gosh Nan, that was a smelly one." Nan would not be amused. As you now know, Nan was never amused. She would growl when other Nans might laugh. She would always tut and look at the ceiling when Timothy's dad told his

Timothy & the Triplets Three

awful jokes. But Timothy didn't worry about his nan's lack of humour, because he remembered overhearing his dad tell his mum that "Nan has lost it", so maybe she had just lost the fun part of her brain.

In fact, the more he thought about it, the more he wondered if it was in her purse because he had never actually seen Nan open her purse. She never paid for anything whilst his mum and dad were around. She would rarely pay for anything when they weren't around. She had coupons and vouchers for everything. Even at Christmas and birthdays there were vouchers everywhere. When he would open his birthday card from his nan, a voucher offering money off thick sliced bread would flutter to the floor.

At school, Timothy's friends would compare how much money they had been given for Christmas and birthdays. Rocky Smith (apparently, he was called Rocky because he was born in Blackpool) was always top of the 'Money-in-the-card league'. Last year, he cashed in over £500. However, the fact his mum and dad had been divorced three times each meant he had four sets of grandparents... so really, he was cheating. Sausage Jones (he was born in Cumbria) came bottom of the league table because his grandad used to glue five new pennies to the inside of the card. Sausage wondered if his grandad was confused and thought that they could be worth more because they were shiny and new. Then there was the sad case of a boy in Timothy's class called 70 Church Road Blackburn. Apparently (and maybe you have already guessed), he was called 70 Church Road Blackburn because he was born in 70 Church Road Blackburn. But his name was not the sad part. He was only given

Timothy & the Triplets Three

money that his big brother (who was called 17 Greenbank Avenue Blackburn because – yes, you've guessed it – he was born in 17 Greenbank Avenue) had printed using the photocopier at work. Timothy felt sorry for him, but 70 Church Road didn't seem to mind about the money – or his name –and said he was glad he was not born in 1 Sweaty Armpit Avenue. The only reason Timothy did not come bottom of the list was because he would lie and pretend he got £10 from his joyless nan, but he never got a penny. He lied because he didn't want to give the bullies any more excuses to make him the butt of their jokes.

School was generally boring, rubbish and horrid when the bullies got hold of him. Timothy's class was made up of lots of different kids – amongst them were the triplets: Eddy, Neddy and Bert Fullofsnot. According to Lulabella, their mum and dad (Mr and Mrs Fullofsnot) made them in a test tube. Timothy's dad said it was cheaper to do it like that. Timothy tried to ask his dad why it was cheaper but he got a very stern look from his mum, so he dropped the subject.

Eddy, Neddy and Bert went everywhere together, including the toilet. Timothy was told it was because they were going to the toilets together to smoke. One day, Timothy was already in the toilets when the triplets came in and he heard them saying they needed to make it look as though they were smoking so that the other kids thought they looked tough. They had brought the contents of the ashtrays from home to rub on their clothes so they would smell authentic.

Even though they spent most of their time bullying people because of how they looked,

Timothy & the Triplets Three

how they spoke or because of what they wore, the triplets were nothing special to look at themselves.

Eddy was short and skinny, and was the owner of the most horrific nose. His nose sort of started at his hairline and then dribbled all the way down his face almost to his chin, where it got wider and more nobbled as it descended his skinny cheeks. But Eddy's real talent was neither his skinniness nor the ugliness of his nose, it was the grotesque, stinking, slimy, dense farts he could drop with an accompanying deep-toned noise whenever he wanted.

Neddy, on the other hand, was tall and walked with his head forward as though he was trying to

Timothy & the Triplets Three

cross the finishing line in a photo finish race. Neddy's talent was punching people in the face. He had practised a lot with Eddy's face (the cause of Eddy's ugly nose) and was considered a champion face puncher.

The third triplet, Bert, was round; he had round hands, a round face and a round tummy. Apart from being round, he did not have an additional talent, he did not have a champion punch, nor did he have a vicious-smelling bottom. Bert was, in fact, soft, daft and dragged down by his two dumb brothers. Timothy sometimes felt sorry for Bert. He thought it must be tough being made

Timothy & the Triplets Three

in the same test tube as Eddy and Neddy and having to hang around with them all the time. But Timothy did not worry about it too much. Timothy's dad said the jeans had got mixed up in the test tubes. (This was a surprise to Timothy as he thought test tubes were very small and nowhere near big enough to hold a pair of jeans, never mind three!) Timothy's mum had told his dad to be quiet unless he had something generous to say. She explained to Timothy that jeans were not the same as genes. Dad would just wink and pretend he didn't know there was a difference. With his head hidden behind the newspaper, Timothy's dad would mutter that he would say something generous about them when he could think of something. He pointed out that the triplets couldn't be very clever if they had to use spray paint to write their names everywhere: "Eddy Neddy Bert woz 'ere." He said they were the sort of people who made spelling mistakes when they had their names tattooed and that soon they would have "Edee, Needy and Barty" written on their arms. He then said he thought they were the best thugs in Timothy's school. Timothy's mum raised an eyebrow. His dad apologised and said that actually, what he meant to say was that there was more brain activity in a cemetery. Mum raised a finger. Timothy's father tried one last time:

"Ok, sorry what I meant to say was they are as thick as two short planks, as daft as a pair of brushes and possibly not human at all."

Timothy & the Triplets Three

After that, Dad was ignored for two full days! However, Dad said it was worth it.

Chapter 5
Ralph the Debt Collector

As you already know, Timothy had a keen interest in making money, and not just the money he expected to get inside his birthday and Christmas cards. He was always on the lookout of how to build up his 'capital' (as he had heard them say on *Dragons' Den*).

He was so keen on money that he set up his first business when he was seven years old. Collecting Lulabella's unloved DVDs in a big box, he would rent them out to unsuspecting

Timothy & the Triplets Three

members of his family. Whilst his day rates for hiring DVDs were reasonable, the overdue charges were punishing. Many a debt was run up by an unsuspecting aunty or cousin who would innocently take three DVDs home only to have to part with £20 when they were returned (unwatched) a week later. Timothy was unforgiving on the payment of overdue fees. "Read the small print," he would insist as they left his house, innocence written all over his face. But upon the return of the overdue items, the innocence had dissolved and 'Ralph the Debt Collector' was in charge.

Ralph was Timothy's alter ego. Whilst Timothy rented out DVDs with a smile and a "Hope you enjoy the movie, Aunty Fixwigs," it was Ralph who collected the debt. Ralph was uncompromising. He'd close his eyes slightly, rub his hands together and lower his voice whilst saying, "Would you really try to steal from a child, Aunty Fixwigs?"

Ralph always had change when his aunties couldn't find it in their deep handbags. He refused to accept I.O.U.'s. However, he was always fair and called people to remind them of their debts. Without fail, Ralph sent statements out in red envelopes and was not interested in excuses and small talk. Pay up or Ralph stays on the case. It was a rare occurrence when someone forgot or refused to pay. On these occasions, as a final attempt to extract the overdue fees, Ralph would remind relatives of the horrible case of cousin Lucy's boyfriend, Stevo.

Cousin Lucy was fun, although Timothy's dad said she was a fashion victim. His dad explained that this was why she bit her nails and then glued false ones on to make it look like she had long nails – or talons, as he called them. The problem was that she would then bite the false nails, but because the glue was so super strong, she could not take the false nails off. So, after a few weeks she would end up with several layers of false nails all on top of each other. Her multi-layered, multi-coloured nails looked like the tentacles of an alien monster. She would also wear shoes with narrow points at the toes and very high heels. This meant she walked like a wobbly hippopotamus and complained her feet were sore all the time. Cousin Lucy had 18 earrings in each ear – Timothy had spent one family meal counting them as they jangled like wind chimes as she ate. Timothy was worried her ears might fall off but they seemed to stay put. She made a lovely jingly noise when she wobbled on her high-heeled shoes.

Timothy liked Cousin Lucy, because even if she was a fashion victim, she would always say funny things to make Timothy laugh. She wore bright red lipstick which she generously shared with everyone she met, hugged and kissed. She waved her hands around wildly when she was telling stories. Sometimes she would giggle and wave her hands around so much that she would completely forget the end of the story.

Stevo, Cousin Lucy's boyfriend, was a very different kettle of fish. (Timothy first heard this saying from his nan, but every time he checked her kettle he never found any fish inside, which

Timothy & the Triplets Three

was most confusing.) Cousin Lucy's boyfriend crossed the line when he rented some of Timothy's DVDs. It was only a couple of DVDs and they were only a few days late, but it was what happened afterwards that caused the trouble. If he had paid up when he was first asked it would have only cost him the price of a pizza and a drink. However, what Stevo did was pat Timothy on the head, smile and slide the DVDs onto the kitchen table without payment. Then he pretended he could not hear Timothy's polite requests for the payment of overdue fees.

He ignored the statements and laughed when Ralph made phone calls to ask for payment. In the end, Ralph pointed out Stevo's non-payment of overdue DVD fees to Cousin Lucy. His reluctance to accept his responsibility (and the fact she had a soft spot for her younger cousin) meant she dumped him. Well, that and the fact that he did not like cats, did not wash his hands when he went to the loo, picked his nose and ate it, sung the wrong words to songs, and Lucy was convinced he wore the same socks every day for 12 weeks.

She was thankful to Timothy (and Ralph) for highlighting this flaw in his personality before it was too late. Timothy did not have the courage to list all the other flaws or to point out that Stevo bit his nails, ate them and pulled the hairs out his nose while talking to you, as though he was invisible.

Timothy & the Triplets Three

To be honest, Cousin Lucy should have spotted he was a loser much more quickly than she did. The signs were there for all to see: dried egg in the corner of his mouth in the mornings, being a supporter of West Snotwich Albion, had never watched XYZ Factor, bad breath, greasy fringe, dandruff, freckles on his toes and he burped when he was nervous. No one is quite sure what became of skinflint boyfriend Stevo; he simply seemed to drift into ex-boyfriend obscurity along with his second-hand scooter, the L-plates always hanging on for grim death with sticky tape.

The only redeeming factor of Boyfriend Stevo was when he ran over the bully triplets on his moped. No one is quite sure what happened, but it would appear that Eddy, Neddy and Bert were walking across the road, practising how to look cool and hard in their CRABz parker coats.

Timothy & the Triplets Three

Along came boyfriend Stevo on his moped. He was going flat out (a full 26 mph). No one is quite sure whether his glasses were steamed up or he was crying his eyes out inside his helmet (after Cousin Lucy chucked him), but he was driving straight at the triplet bullies. Eddy, Neddy and Bert continued practising being cool and hard, so ignored Boyfriend Stevo hurtling towards them at speed. Timothy was watching from his bedroom window. From the corner of his eye, he could see his dad walking home from work, looking at his feet as always and not paying attention to anything else going on around him.

The first impact was when Stevo smashed into Eddy. The chrome wing mirror caught the triplet's left arm, spinning him around and sending him flying into a hedge, but not before he knocked Neddy into the direct path of the moped. Neddy was struck directly on both his knees. It must have hurt because he let out a loud shriek and started shouting for his 'Mummykins'. (Timothy thought Mummykins was a strange name for his mum, but maybe Neddy was not quite as big and strong as he made out.) By now, Stevo must have been aware of what was happening and tried to twist out of the way by turning to the left. But then Bert tripped (because he wasn't looking where he was going and was instead wondering what his brother was doing in the hedge) and landed to the right at just the moment when Boyfriend Stevo started to pick up speed. They crashed but it didn't have much of an impact on Bert because his roundness caused him to bounce off the moped, knocking him clean off his feet. He was completely lifted off the ground. He sort of spun and landed on his face. Boyfriend Stevo had enough momentum to keep going and waved as he escaped the scene.

Up in his bedroom, Timothy could not stop laughing. He knew he shouldn't but he couldn't help it. After all, the triplets had already caused a lot of pain to others over their few years on this earth. Eddy was bruised and battered and was trying to crawl out of the hedge, Neddy lay on the ground crying for his Mummykins and Bert

Timothy & the Triplets Three

was rolling around with his round hands over his round face, howling.

Further down the road, Timothy's dad had eventually lifted his gaze from his shoes when he heard the commotion of Eddy landing in the hedge and had dashed over to help, but he had been run over by Stevo making a swift exit. This stopped Timothy's laughter and he screamed as he saw his dad land on the road clutching his foot.

Mum called an ambulance and they all spent the night in A&E. Everyone was ok (sort of). Eddy had a broken arm and had it put in plaster. Neddy had a large bandage on both his knees and left the hospital on crutches. Bert had a few stitches over his eye, a broken nose and a nasty graze on his right leg.

Mr and Mrs Fullofsnot arrived late in the evening to see their sons. Apparently, they had

Timothy & the Triplets Three

been out at the Northern Underground Members of the Personal Training Interest Evening and Supper Group. (NUMPTIES)

Timothy had felt anxious at the hospital. There in front of him were three of the bullies who made his life a misery. Part of him wanted to jump with joy and celebrate every yelp and groan as they wept in pain. But Timothy's big heart meant he also felt some compassion and concern. However, even with them in their delicate state, Timothy was scared of them.

Timothy & the Triplets Three

Mr and Mrs Fullofsnot were worried about their darling sons and not paying much attention to what was going on around them, but even they could sense the strange atmosphere as Timothy's mum tried to coax him out of the hospital broom cupboard from where he was whispering questions to find out about the triplets' injuries.

As he peered out at Mr and Mrs Fullofsnot's quizzical faces, Timothy was almost tempted to ask them if it was at all possible for their sons to ease up on him and not make his life quite so miserable. But he didn't think it would work because Timothy had heard rumours about Mr Fullofsnot's past and, given what he had heard, he thought Mr Fullofsnot would be proud of his boys' bullying behavior. One day, he hoped they could find some way to stop the bully war because the bullies were winning 127– nil.

Timothy & the Triplets Three

The triplets went home that night but Dad was kept in for an operation on his foot, which was broken in three places. No one mentioned that they knew Stevo because the police were asking lots of questions about the driver of the moped. Stevo would not survive in prison, and despite his reluctance to pay Timothy's DVD fine, no-one wanted to cause him harm.

Timothy never saw Boyfriend Stevo again. But Stevo did drop an envelope through the door containing the remaining and final £1.27 outstanding DVD hire fees that he owed.

Chapter 6
Lulabella Queen of America

It wasn't only Timothy who was interested in money in his family. But whereas Timothy liked to make money, Lulabella liked to spend it. Lulabella liked expensive things: Jinny Shoo Shoes, Cross Channel Bags and obviously, Colex Watches. When she ran out of cash she would hunt down anything in the house which could be sold by Timothy on Dbay, the online market place for young people to sell stuff and get cash. The site had the added benefit that the money

Timothy & the Triplets Three

you made could be spent on getting more stuff you wanted, which you could sell again in a few months when you got bored of it.

One day, Lulabella scooped up three of her T-shirts, two pairs of Dad's shorts, four old perfumes from Mum's recycling box and a signed rugby shirt from an England player called Gluckbobby Butnedefi. Lulabella guessed Gluckbobby Butnedefi was not his real name but the writing was so bad that she could not make out what his real name was. Also, Lulabella had washed the rugby shirt the previous week by mistake and half the signature had been washed away, so she really could not make out the name of the high-profile rugby player. She did consider whether she could use one of her Sharpies to write it back on.

Timothy & the Triplets Three

But Lulabella saved her best money making ideas for when she moved to her university in America. She realised that Americans loved her English accent. They all wanted to know if she was friends with the Queen (she said they were best friends). Americans assumed she lived in a castle. She didn't try to change their minds because she had visited a castle on a school trip when she was 7 years old and liked the thought of having a bedroom in a turret. Such was the interest in Lulabella that she was known as 'That English Girl Who Knows the Queen'.

One day, Lulabella's mum sent her a special hamper of her favourite foods to cheer her up.

Timothy & the Triplets Three

She was a long way from home and sometimes she got homesick, so she sent her a box full of:

Bovril

Cadbury's Flake

Blackpool rock

Black pudding

Scones

Baked beans

HP Sauce

Iron Bru

Mint Imperials

Sherbet Lemons

And a whole load more of her favourite comfort foods. When Lulabella's university friends came to visit her in her dormitory they all tried some of her mum's gifts from England. They loved the food and (this is the best bit) they wanted more, and more and more. So Lulabella started to take

Timothy & the Triplets Three

orders for foods and then email the order though to her mum. She didn't explain to her mum that she was selling the food to her friends, but this was ok because her mum was so pleased she was eating well, and cleaning her teeth, and wrapping up warm and was always in bed by 8.00pm. (Ok, the last bit was not completely true, but it was what Lulabella told her parents.)

This gave birth to the Lulabella Food Company, earning her lots of cash to spend on improving her collection of shoes, boots, bags, watches and perfume.

Although Timothy liked to make money, he wasn't miserly about spending it and was proud that he could afford good presents for his family. Timothy's dad's birthday was fast approaching. His dad was really excited because he hoped that he would continue to get lots of sympathy for his broken foot. He was disappointed that no one had mentioned it for a while, despite him letting out a loud "Oh" or "Argh" every so often to remind people that he was injured.

Timothy had bought his dad a Lego Mini Car kit. He was so thrilled because he knew his dad would love it. The previous year, he had bought him a Lego Space Rocket and it had taken both of them eight months to make. He loved working on Lego kits with his dad because they would just sit for hours chatting about everything and laughing at the daft things they would say. When they were constructing the landing gear on the spacecraft, Dad said to Timothy that he would like to know just how hairy Mrs Whitehead's legs were.

Mrs Whitehead was the biology teacher at Timothy's school. The rumour was she got her name because of all the little white-headed spots she had on her face. They really stood out because of her very red cheeks. However, Timothy's mum was shocked when he mentioned this to her one day after school. She said in no uncertain terms that Mrs Whitehead had that name because she was married to Mr Whitehead, who worked in the bank. Mrs Whitehead's ears were so small that she was unable to wear earrings, so she had a stud in her nose. This was awkward because when she got a cold, snot would dribble out of the nose stud and down her pointy chin. One day in late spring, Mrs Whitehead had to cover for the

Timothy & the Triplets Three

history teacher who was having root canal work at the dentist. During the lesson, Mrs Whitehead was suffering from hay fever. She was rubbing her eyes and there was a constant stream of green snot running out of her nose. Every five minutes she would reach into her old leather satchel and pull out a paper hanky to blow her nose. By the end of the lesson the wastepaper bin at the side of her desk was full of soggy snot-filled hay fever lava-encrusted tissues. Just as the lesson finished, she let out a loud wailing noise and grabbed the end of her nose as she realised she had not only cleared her nose, but also blown her nose stud out. As the children filed out of the class, Mrs Whitehead could be seen kneeling on the classroom floor digging through a bin full of dripping snot-filled paper hankies, squeezing each one tightly to locate the lost nose stud.

Timothy & the Triplets Three

One other fact about Mrs Whitehead was that she had the hairiest legs Timothy had ever seen. So, as Timothy and his dad moved on to constructing the nose cone of the Lego Space Rocket, Dad proposed that the hairs would keep her warm in the winter and Timothy said that her legs were hairier than a donkey's legs. Dad almost fell off his chair laughing. He tried to talk but was laughing too much. Eventually he started making noises like a donkey and had tears running down his face. At that moment, Timothy's mum came in and asked what all the laughing was about. Dad tried to explain what was funny but Timothy's mum did not laugh so they both tried to stifle their giggles. When Timothy's mum finally went out to take Mrs Kingspan to her manicure appointment, they both let out a huge laugh.

Timothy & the Triplets Three

You may be asking yourself why Mrs Kingspan needed a lift to her manicure appointment? Well, the truth is she was unable to drive herself because for the last 14 years and 7 months she had been growing her fingernails so that she could be in the Big Book of Records for the longest nails in the world. Her nails were 65 cm long, which was long enough. However, the world record was held by an Australian snail farmer, whose nails were 123 cm long. She had grown them to pull snails out of their shell on the snail farm which she shared with her sister. Her sister held the Big Book of Records award for the longest hairs in her nose. The black nose hairs were now 204 cm long and had to be tied up on the side of her head, which meant she could not hear anything. As far as anyone knew, there was no benefit to having long nose hairs on a snail farm.

When Timothy's father told him the story of the Australian snail farmers, that started another wave of hysterical laughter. They were laughing so hard it started a fit of hiccups.

On reflection, it was not surprising the Lego Space Rocket took so long to make.

That night, Timothy started his 'normal' routine of getting ready for bed, making sure he brushed his teeth for eight minutes. He did this three times a day. Other parts of his routine included eating five portions of fruit and vegetables a day, 30 minutes' exercise, 60 minutes' homework, kid's yoga for 30 minutes and playing 12 minutes of his computer game before going to bed by 8.30pm. As he brushed his teeth, he was tempted by his dad's suggestion to get a photograph of Mrs Whitehead's hairy legs and send them off to the Big Book of Records. However, he couldn't work out how he would do it.

Chapter 7
Dad's surprise birthday cake

When Timothy's dad had to pop out to go to the physio on his foot the next day, his mum said they should start making Dad's Surprise Birthday Cake. Dad always got a Surprise Birthday Cake for his birthday. Sometimes the surprise came in the shape of a mixing spoon that Mum left in the mixture by mistake, sometimes the cake was a surprise when she swapped the 100ml of brandy for 1 litre of brandy and Dad slept for most of his birthday! One time, it was a surprise because it tasted wonderful and looked glorious. Dad said that that cake had been the biggest surprise of all. There was one year when the Surprise Birthday Cake appeared in October… but Timothy's dad's birthday was in July. No matter what ingredient Mum left out (or added), she always put loads of love into it. Timothy was the best at mixing love into Dad's cakes and so always had the last stir.

Dad loved cake, especially homemade cake. Lulabella always made Dad her famous lemon drizzle cake when she was home. It was amazing! It tasted so good that Dad had been known to eat a whole lemon drizzle cake on the day it was made. When Mum would ask where the rest of the cake was, he would blame the dog – which made everyone laugh because they didn't have a dog. Lulabella once made Dad a super big lemon drizzle cake. In fact, it was so big the drizzle drizzled all down the sides of the cake, down the plate and onto the kitchen unit. It then drizzled down the kitchen door and onto the kitchen floor. The drizzle kept drizzling until it made it out into the hall, onto Mum's favourite Indian rug. By the time Lulabella had noticed what was happening, it had drizzled itself out the front door and halfway down the street to the Butcher's shop. It was described on the front page of the Green Town Gazette as a 'tsunami of unstoppable lemon drizzle icing'.

Timothy wished Lulabella was home to cook her famous lemon drizzle cake for Dad's birthday but she was busy climbing a mountain somewhere on the other side of the world. In previous years when she had been in the country, Lulabella had come back from university to celebrate her dad's birthday – and also to ask her mum to wash some clothes, borrow some loo roll, check out Mum's shoes, feed herself, get her feet pedicured, repair her sunglasses, fix her teeth retainer, download some movies, swap her headphones for Timothy's, catch up with friends and ask Dad to pay a few credit card bills she had picked up. Timothy wished he could tell Lulabella about the bullies because she would march around to the Fullofsnots house and wipe the floor with them. But even if she had been around, the next day she would be back at university and he would be alone again, facing the three Fullofsnots on his own.

Traditionally, Timothy would always help his mum make Dad's Surprise Birthday Cake, but this time he was distracted because he was only half way through 'Teachers vs Zombies version 36'. It was his new video game on his Z-Cube 950c. When his mum asked for help, he explained that he was just up to the best bit where the teachers had their brains eaten if they failed the maths test. Timothy knew they were going to fail the maths test because Mr Shouty, the sports teacher, was on the team and Timothy knew he couldn't even count his own fingers. Twice last year he selected 12 people for the football team; it was so embarrassing! So he pleaded with his mum and asked if he could just carry on playing the game until the zombies had completely eaten the teacher's brains. His mum turned a little bit green then smiled (because she knew most of the teachers at Timothy's school behaved as though they had already had their brains eaten). She said it was fine and she would make a start on mixing

Timothy & the Triplets Three

Dad's birthday cake whilst giving Cousin Lucy a ring to catch up on her news.

Cousin Lucy always had news and last week her news was all about her new boyfriend. Lucy described him as 6 foot 2 inches, slim, an athlete, a successful singer in a band, world record F1 driver, great tan, blue eyes, clean fingernails, qualified pilot and he was fluent in Australian. Timothy's mum said he sounded amazing. Lucy said, "He will be amazing if I can just find him."

As Timothy continued to slay zombie teachers, he could hear his mum on the phone with Cousin Lucy. She had put the phone on hands-free so she could prepare the cake's ingredients, which meant that Timothy could hear the conversation. They were laughing about how Cousin Lucy had dyed a customer's hair blonde, but when they washed the dye out, the hair had turned out blue.

Apparently, the customer was delighted when she saw it and gave her an extra large tip.

As Cousin Lucy started a story about another customer, Timothy's mum started to weigh the flour and the butter and count the eggs. Cousin Lucy described how she had knocked a woman's false leg off and it had rolled around the shop. Timothy heard his mum giggling as she put the ingredients in the electric mixer and switched it on, then carried on her phone call as it started to beat the ingredients together. To begin with, it started off slowly whilst Cousin Lucy described the new colour she had applied to her multi-layered nails.

However, as she was describing the neon pink shade she was planning on using next, Timothy came into the kitchen. The zombie brain-fest was over and he wanted to help make the Surprise Birthday Cake. The sight that greeted him was a bit of a shock. There was his mum with her mixer whizzing around in the bowl at 100mph. But it wasn't mixing anything much as the cake mix was up the wall and all over the big stainless steel fridge. His mum did not seem to have noticed. Gently, he tapped her on the shoulder and, when she turned around to look at Timothy – who was pointing at the cake splatter which was now everywhere – she let out a yelp and dropped Cousin Lucy into the remaining cake mix in the bowl. Timothy stood with his eyes wide open, then started licking the cake splatter off the big stainless steel fridge. Timothy's mum managed to stop her mixer from whizzing around the bowl like some sort of spinning alien beast by pulling the plug out of the wall. It stopped just as a large dollop of cake mix dropped onto her nose from the ceiling.

Timothy & the Triplets Three

Then they both started laughing. Timothy had caught his breath and was just about to ask his mum what on earth she was doing when they heard a distorted burble from the mixing bowl. It was Cousin Lucy wanting to know what was going on. That set them off into another burst of uncontrollable laughter.

"How on earth did that happen?" Timothy asked as he stared at his mum's mixer, wondering if it was plugged into a special electrical socket. His mum was busy wiping down the phone handset with a tea towel, having hung up on Cousin Lucy with a quick "Tell you later." Then Timothy suddenly remembered that his dad had changed the fuse in the mixer when Father Mike needed a fuse for his quadrophonic karaoke. A stunned Timothy's mum stood looking at her mixer, then looking at the mixing bowl, then looking at the cake mix – which was now decorating most the kitchen walls, floor and ceiling – then back to the mixing bowl.

Once she had recovered from her shock, they both started to clean up the kitchen, eating the chocolate chips from the mixture because it would be an awful waste to throw them into the bin. After a while, Timothy felt sick and decided it would be much better to put them in the bin with the rest of the mix.

Although Timothy felt he had to explain that Dad changing the fuse may have had something to do with it, he could not work out how to mention this to his mum without his dad being sent to the dog house for weeks and weeks and weeks. As she did not have a clue, he thought he should probably leave it that way.

Mum decided to have a second attempt at the cake and, with Timothy's help, carefully measured out the flour, eggs, milk and cherries. The latter was a substitute as all the chocolate chips had gone. All was going well until his mum switched the mixer on again. Slowly, bit-by-bit, she turned up the speed of the mixer. The ingredients were mixing well when, after about a minute, the mixer started to whisk faster and faster. His mum looked at her mixer and then looked at Timothy. The apprehensive look on her face made Timothy a little scared. They watched the mixing bowl bounce around on the kitchen work surface. Timothy suggested they may need to slow it down. His mum agreed, but even though she turned the dial to zero, the mixer kept getting faster. Faster and faster, the mixture in the bowl was beaten until lumps of cake mixture started leaving the bowl and heading for the ceiling.

This time, the clean up took several hours and was only just completed before Dad came back home very tired and sore from the physio.

Chapter 8
Mr Yeastly bakes

After this messy second attempt, Timothy managed to convince his mum that this year's Surprise Birthday Cake for his dad would be a surprise because it would be made by Mr Yeastly, their neighbour, who was a baking sensation. (Cousin Lucy could not believe that Timothy's mum had cakes made by the star of *I'm a Cook, Bake Me Out of Here*, but it was true.)

When you knocked at Mr Yeastly's door it would always take him a while to answer it. Timothy thought this must be because Mr Yeastly enjoyed a few too many of his own cakes. He was small, round and smelt of cinnamon.

When he was at his cooker, he had a little old battered wooden box he stood on so he could reach the top shelf. His shoes were always covered in flour and he usually had flour in his hair and flour on his face. His kitchen was a graveyard to every kitchen gadget that had ever been advertised on TV.

There was no doubt he had a weakness for buying kitchen gadgets. He had tried to start a support group locally – Kitchen Gadget Buying Anonymous – but it had ended up with him sitting in Father Mike's church hall with a lady from the next village chatting about kitchen gadgets for hours, getting more and more excited about buying a new banana peeler, or the new currant slicer, or the very tempting automatic jam spreader for toasted crumpets. The problem was that after two hours of thinking and talking about his kitchen gadget buying addiction, he would go straight home, switch on the TV and buy all the new gadgets that he had just learnt about from his fellow kitchen gadget collector. He did not know the name of the lady from the next village because she had said she wanted to stay anonymous.

Amongst some of his worst gadgets he had bought was one that made sausages from any leftovers. It was called the 'Express Bubble and Squeak Sausage Maker'. You kept all the food scraps throughout the week and then fed them into the Express Bubble and Squeak Sausage Maker. The gadget squished and squashed all the leftovers together and then you added flavours like curry or egg & garlic, peanut butter & mint, or Timothy's favourite, strawberry & hot pepper. The flavour went some way to hide the fact the sausages were made from the leftover food from the previous week, but never quite managed to disguise it. After lots of mixing and mashing, the sausages came out of the end of the gadget. Once, Timothy had asked Mr Yeastly why it was the worst gadget he had bought. Mr Yeastly just pointed at the toilet and held his nose then shook his head.

Then there was a gadget that was supposed to make the perfect beetroot, garlic and custard omelette in 30 seconds. Mr Yeastly said it took hours and it was anything but perfect – even Mrs Fixwig's cat refused to taste it.

Timothy & the Triplets Three

When Timothy once spent an afternoon with Mr Yeastly, trying to learn his baking secrets, he noticed a machine called 'The Big Breakfast in a Bun'. It promised to cook bacon, egg, cheese, sausage and a bread bun all together in three minutes. The contraption was about the size of a kettle and had lots of openings, flaps, slots and gaps where various parts of the big breakfast would be inserted. The bottom of the bread roll went in at the bottom, then the next flap allowed you to insert bacon, then the next drawer opened to allow you to break an egg and drop it inside, then there was a gap for cheese, a slot for sausage and finally, at the top, was the last flap for the top of the bread roll. Once you had inserted each ingredient you closed up all the flaps, slots, drawers and gaps. You poured tomato or brown sauce in the top, plugged it

Timothy & the Triplets Three

in and switched the machine on. The timer ticked away for three minutes as it played 'Oh what a beautiful morning'. You could hear the sizzle, splotch and splatter as various parts of the 'Big Breakfast in a Bun' were heated up, fried, melted, toasted and hopefully cooked. Finally, with a triumphant PING, the cooking was done. The flaps were removed carefully and out would slide the 'magnificent' concoction. Mr Yeastly confessed that, whilst the picture on the box looked tasty, the result was not quite as picturesque. He explained he had always ended up wearing more of 'The Big Breakfast in a Bun' than he had ever eaten and, although it did only take three minutes to cook, it took three hours to wash the gadget afterwards.

Amongst the deceased kitchen gadgets in his kitchen were shelves full of cookery books and magazines. He had many books by Prince Humphrey of Denmark, the famed cook who had a very popular cookery programme on primetime TV called *How to Eat like a Great Dane.* Prince Humphrey of Denmark's signature dish was Pickled Duck with Parmesan Apricots.

Unfortunately, Prince Humphrey of Denmark's career had gone off the rails when the local chip shop sold their story to the Moon Daily newspaper. Timothy's dad had called it a "Chips and Tell" story. Apparently, Prince Humphrey of Denmark had rarely eaten his own cooking for years. Prince Humphrey of Denmark hated his own food and had run up quite a large credit account at the

Timothy & the Triplets Three

fish and chip shop around the corner from his house. Because Prince Humphrey of Denmark had sunk all his money into a MeTube internet video channel called 'How to Cook Great Dane Food for Your Elderly Step Grandmother', which crashed and burnt and only ever had 2 viewers (and those were his parents), he was unable to pay his chip shop bill. He had been building up a substantial debt, always telling them to "add it on the tab" because he had to get out quickly before he was recognised.

After many attempts from the chip shop owner to arrange a reasonable repayment plan with Prince Humphrey of Denmark (as well as a 'pay as you eat plan'), the chip shop owner eventually had to accept his money was not going to get paid. One night, in the chip shop, the owner was moaning about the unpaid account to a customer who turned out to be a reporter at the Moon Daily Newspaper. The rest is history. Prince Humphrey of Denmark's waistline was a national talking point for weeks; his books were ceremonially burned by the Women's Institute in Bradford, his TV series was ditched by Nosh TV and the Food Channel. Even his charity appearance on *Comical Food For Fun Day* was cancelled for fear the audience would boo him. It also turned out that he was not really Danish, but had been born in Cornwall and his real name was John Toad. In the newspaper article and the series of TV interviews on the back of it, the chip shop owner had revealed Prince Humphrey of Denmark's love for battered cod and chips with mushy peas, all of which had to be delivered to the back of the block of flats so nobody would know of his secret.

Timothy & the Triplets Three

Timothy was not sure, but rumours suggested that Prince Humphrey of Denmark was planning on opening his own fish and chip shop in an effort to bounce back onto the food scene. Although the police still wanted to talk to him about a possible crime he had been involved with which related to cruelty to chicken fried rice. The police said their investigation continues.

Timothy wanted to tell Mr Yeastly about his mum's mixer going out of control, how it had started to whisk cakes at 100 mph and how his mum did not even know about it until she had covered the kitchen, including the stainless steel fridge, with cake splatter. But he decided to say nothing and stay silent. He felt it might be better to keep it as one of those family secrets which is never discussed outside the family.

Timothy & the Triplets Three

Dad had explained to him about keeping family secrets one Sunday when he farted in church. Although Timothy heard nothing and his dad continued to listen to Father Mike with an innocent look on his face, it was an SBD (Silent But Deadly) fart. The smell was awful; the old lady in front of them with blue hair had fainted due to the rotten stench of the previous night's curry with curdled blue cheese dressing. The only good thing was that when she came round in Father Mike's front room, she could only remember fainting and not Timothy dad's farting. Timothy suggested to his dad that he should own up as the phantom farter but his dad persuaded him that some things were best kept in the family.

"No good will come of confessing to Father Mike that I farted and made the old lady faint," he had said.

Timothy & the Triplets Three

Father Mike had been part way through his sermon when Dad farted. He had been telling the congregation that he had been in the barber's shop to ask them to trim the long hairs sticking out of his ears. Something had clearly gone wrong because when he emerged he had a skull and crossbones tattooed onto his hand. Timothy wondered why Father Mike had not asked why the barber was working on his hand to get rid of his ear hair and was just about to ask his father when the SBD happened. Father Mike showed his tattoo to the congregation and explained he had no recollection of getting it done and then broke into singing 'Fifteen Men on a Dead Man's Chest' just as the old lady with blue hair fainted.

As Timothy thought back to that Sunday, he decided to keep the family secret about Mum's mixer and instead smiled sweetly at Mr Yeastly.

Timothy & the Triplets Three

Timothy enjoyed talking to Mr Yeastly. He was kind and caring, and had confided in Timothy that his love for baking was a way of coping with the bullying he had experienced in his life. Mr Yeastly told Timothy that when he went to school he had been bullied by local thugs Smasher and Grabber. Timothy was amazed to find out years later that Smasher's real name was Arnold Fullofsnot, the triplets' father.

During their chats, Mr Yeastly made a point of reminding Timothy that, as bad as bullies were, they were usually unhappy in their lives. He encouraged Timothy to never give up and reassured him that he would find a way to sort out those horrid boys.

Once Timothy had explained about needing some cake for his dad's birthday (while keeping the family secret about the mixer to himself), Mr

Yeastly parcelled up eight double chocolate and cherry muffins, a sherry and cucumber trifle, a coffee and walnut slice, four vanilla scones with cinnamon and, finally, his fabulous mint wafer and cold tea sponge cake. Timothy stood, arms outstretched, whilst Mr Yeastly loaded him up with goodies. Finally, he stuffed a white chocolate and beef gravy cookie in Timothy's pocket because he knew it was his favourite. Mr Yeastly winked and put his hand on his heart as he said goodbye.

As Timothy left through the front door, he stepped over a huge pile of yet to be opened cookery magazines on the doormat that had come in the post. Each one was bursting with new recipes promising to be lower in fat, chocolatier than last month's recipe, or cooked and on the table in 10 minutes, and costing only 50p to make. The one on the top of the pile announced that it included 1001 great things to do with rice, and the one peeking out beneath it even had a headline promising to "Help you lose those extra few pounds off your hips". Timothy was the first to admit that he did not know much about cooking, but he doubted there was a recipe that could help you lose weight off your hips.

Chapter 9
Triplets ruin a birthday

On his way back from his visits, Timothy usually managed to squash one of Mr Yeastly's delights and this day was no exception. Just as he reached the gate of his house, something rushed past him, knocking him off his feet. He tripped and stumbled into the gate, spun around, and almost dropped the mint wafer and cold tea sponge cake but grabbed it just in time. However, he fell backwards and managed to sit on all four of the vanilla scones with cinnamon. As he was

Timothy & the Triplets Three

catching his breath, Timothy was lifted roughly off the floor by Neddy and Eddy, who opened the box of scones, took one out, then rubbed it vigorously into Timothy's white, fluffy hair. Bert tried to stop them, suggesting that they should just steal the cakes and eat them, but Neddy had a much better idea, a very cruel idea. Each of Mr Yeastly's cakes was removed from its box and then forced into Timothy's mouth. First, they crammed each of the eight double chocolate and cherry muffins into his face, then the three remaining vanilla scones with cinnamon and, finally, Mr Yeastly's fabulous mint wafer and cold tea sponge cake. A coffee and walnut slice was pushed into his ears and the sherry and cucumber trifle was slipped down the back of his shirt. Eventually, after much triplet laughter, Timothy was left slumped in his garden, covered in (and full of) cake.

Timothy & the Triplets Three

Any other day, he would have just accepted that this was the bully triplets' idea of fun – but not this day. This was a big, special family day, his dad's birthday. Now the triplets had, once again, spoilt his day. Not only had they spoilt his day, but because they had ruined all the cake, they had spoilt his dad's birthday. He felt defeated and hopeless. On what should be a happy occasion, Timothy sat covered in cake and wondered if his life would ever be free of this terrible triplet torment.

Timothy & the Triplets Three

Bert sneaked back after his two brothers where gone. He said he was sorry and helped Timothy get home. Timothy noticed that he was still limping and had lost weight, probably as a result of the collision with Stevo. Although Bert was not as bad as his two grotesque brothers, this did not mean Bert was able to stop them. If only Timothy could find a way to increase Bert's confidence so that he could stop the bullying they delivered to so many of his friends at school.

Before he could do anything like that, Timothy had to work out how he could sneak into his house, get washed and changed and beg Mr Yeastly to make some fresh cakes for his dad. Just at the moment he was about to turn the door handle ever so slowly to creep into the house, he heard someone walk along the pavement outside. The footsteps came towards the gate and then up the path. Timothy froze; he desperately did not want to go another 15 rounds with the triplets. But when he wiped the custard away from his eyes, he gulped, because there in front of him stood his Uncle Fingers (this wasn't his real name, but he is still wanted by the police for the hold up at the local watch shop so had taken on this nickname to keep a low profile – he could get lovely watches very cheap.)

Uncle Fingers did not recognise Timothy at first and shouted at the cake-covered lump to get out of his sister's front garden. However, once Timothy opened his mouth and said a tearful hello, Uncle Fingers realised it was Timothy's voice. Uncle Fingers asked him why he was covered in cake and Timothy explained that he had just slipped and spilt the cake over himself. There was a silence as Uncle Fingers looked

Timothy & the Triplets Three

Timothy up and down, from his coffee icing-filled ears to his trifle-covered shoes.

Then Uncle Fingers shook his head and hugged his cake-covered nephew, looked him in his custard-splattered eyes and said gently, "Don't try to kid a kidder. I don't believe you. Tell me what really happened. I am your uncle, your mate, and I will get this sorted for you. But if you don't tell me I will go and get your mum and dad and you will have to tell all of us what has happened."

Timothy dreaded the idea of telling Uncle Fingers what had happened for fear that he would go off and sort out the triplets in a way that would only make things worse. He pleaded with Uncle Fingers to promise that he would treat the information confidentially, and he agreed.

When Timothy had finished his sorry tale, he thought he could almost see a tear

Timothy & the Triplets Three

in Uncle Fingers' eye. However, what Timothy didn't realise was that the tear was not sadness. The tear in Uncle Fingers' eyes was rage.

Uncle Fingers helped Timothy clean up some of the mess. He then caused a distraction by knocking on the front door and greeting his sister with a big hug before pushing his way inside. While everyone was in the kitchen catching up with Uncle Fingers, Timothy slipped straight upstairs, dived into the shower, and got washed and changed.

A quick call to Mr Yeastly sorted the other problem and he delivered yet more amazing cakes, sneaking in through next door's back garden to hand over the still-warm package over the fence to Timothy. No one suspected anything.

Uncle Fingers had come to visit Dad on his birthday because he had been away and he wanted to pop in to see how everyone was doing. He went away quite a lot, although it was rarely his fault. This last time he had to go away because Denis the Driver had forgotten to fill up the getaway car with petrol when they were 'borrowing' some money from the local building society.

Apparently, the actual hold up had gone well. The Minion outfit was perfect; no one had suspected that Uncle Fingers was inside. He was able to hide the money the cashier had given him inside the outfit. However, getting out of the building society in the Minion outfit and into Denis's getaway car was much more difficult. Eventually, he had been bundled into the back of the car successfully, but Denis only made it half-way down the high street before he ran out of fuel. The police were on the scene very quickly. It only gave Uncle Fingers just enough time to wriggle out of the Minion outfit, hide the money under the car seat and then tell the policeman that he had been kidnapped by Denis. Denis was not very bright, otherwise he would have filled the car with petrol. Therefore, Denis happily agreed that he had worn the Minion outfit and kidnapped Uncle Fingers.

It had taken two days at the police station to finalise Denis's confession statement. Uncle Fingers had escaped the long arm of the law again. Denis did not mind because the prison

Timothy & the Triplets Three

they were sending him to always did a special fishy Friday supper with beans, gravy and mushy peas. As a precaution, Uncle Fingers had laid low in case Denis changed his mind while in prison (maybe the fish and chips weren't as good as they used to be) and decided to tell the police a different story. Anyway, that was a month ago, and Uncle Fingers believed that the coast was now clear, so it was safe to visit his family.

Mum was pleased to see Uncle Fingers because she worried when he was away. Sometimes he had been away for six months, but usually it was only for a few weeks. The second time Uncle Fingers had gone away, Timothy's dad had explained to Timothy that when his mum said he was "away" it actually meant he was staying at Her Majesty's pleasure (or prison, as it was known on the street). Timothy thought this must be brilliant. If prison was at Her Majesty's pleasure then it must be very grand. He imagined huge golden sofas, massive 10-metre TVs, ice skating rings, free purple candyfloss, marble pillars, orchestras playing all day and chocolate dipped strawberries.

When Uncle Fingers was away for a long time, Timothy's mum would go and visit him in prison. Timothy had accompanied his mum once to visit him in Sage Wood Prison, which was about 30 miles away.

When they arrived at the prison, Timothy was quite taken aback. The walls were really high with razor wire on the top. The front gates looked small in comparison to the size of the walls. Within the large front gates was a small door that you knocked on to go inside the prison.

Once inside, the colourful world of Sage Wood Village suddenly turned into the completely grey world of Sage Wood Prison. Grey walls, grey front gate, grey ceilings, grey floors and grey doors, grey prison staff uniforms, even the people looked grey. Very grey.

Timothy had never expected prison to be quite so grey. He had imagined dark, scary criminals with scars on their face, bad teeth, staring black eyes, very long arms, long, dirty fingernails and a limp. (The limp would have come from the shotgun wound they suffered during a huge bank robbery.) The prisoners hardly smiled and most snarled. They moved around like the ghosts of people who used to have a personality and a sense of humour. Timothy wondered where all the bullies who had been caught, prosecuted and jailed were kept. He did not see any wings set aside for bullies, which was strange because he would have thought there were thousands of them in the prison. Maybe bullies don't ever get caught, maybe they are brilliant at escaping, or maybe no one cared what bullies got up to.

Before Timothy could meet Uncle Fingers in the prison, he had to pass through a metal detector with his mum and open his bag for a full search. Presumably they were looking for a hacksaw that Uncle Fingers could use to saw his way through the bars on his prison cell windows.

Timothy was expecting to visit Uncle Fingers in his cell, but when the moment came to meet him, he was shown into a grey canteen with tables set out so that each family could sit and talk to their wayward son, brother, Dad, uncle or stepdad. Eventually, after a long wait, the prisoners were marched single file into the grey

Timothy & the Triplets Three

canteen. Uncle Fingers was the last to enter the room. His head was down and he shuffled to their table. Timothy thought he must have shackles around his ankles as he had seen in TV movies. He was really worried. Had prison broken Uncle Fingers? Was he being beaten night and day? Had they used some awful form of electrical brain treatment to brainwash him? As he reached the table, he fell over, did a forward roll, jumped up like a starfish and hugged Timothy and his mum whilst laughing at the top of his voice. Uncle Fingers said he had seen Willy Wonka do it once in a film and he had always wanted to do it. Timothy heaved a sigh of relief and Timothy's mum made a 'tut tut tut' noise, shook her head and raised her eyes to the grey ceiling. The grey prison staff warned Uncle Fingers to keep the noise down so he did.

Timothy & the Triplets Three

Uncle Fingers said he was enjoying his time in prison. The food was good, they had satellite TV, table tennis, five-a-side and he had developed a side-line in telling fortunes by palm reading to earn money from the prisoners and some of the dafter grey prison staff.

"I didn't know you could tell people's fortunes by reading their palms," said Timothy.

"Oh yes," replied Uncle Fingers, "it's always been in the family. Our mum could do it and our grandmother could do it." Timothy's mum scowled and shook her head. "Look Timothy," said Uncle Fingers, "they want to know their future because they don't like their current situation. They want something good to happen to them and they want to believe that tomorrow is going to be better. So, I tell them that tomorrow is going to be better, they will win the lottery, drive a Rolls-Royce. They love it and they love me."

Timothy did not know if he was teasing and his face must have looked uncertain. So, Uncle Fingers asked Timothy for his hand and said he would tell his fortune. Timothy agreed but his mum was mortified, quietly 'tut tutting' under her breath.

Timothy & the Triplets Three

Uncle Fingers said, "You are a bright young man with a very exciting future. You are very much loved by your family. Your mum thinks the world of you. Although you have been through a tough patch, things are about to get much better. You want to play for Neverton one day and you will. You will get great results at your exams and meet a tall, dark, beautiful girl and fall madly in love."

At this point, Timothy went very red in the face and his mum pulled his hand away from Uncle Fingers' grasp. She said to Uncle Fingers it was a shame he couldn't tell his own fortune otherwise he would have known the CCTV was watching him when he tried to borrow the jewellery from the shop at the end of our road, then he would not be sat in prison today.

Timothy asked Uncle Fingers where the massive TV was and the free candyfloss and what time the orchestra would play? Uncle Fingers looked confused. Timothy explained that his dad had told him Uncle Fingers was staying at Her Majesty's pleasure and he knew that Her Majesty would have free candyfloss, a massive TV and an all-day orchestra. Uncle Fingers nodded, put his finger on his lips and made a quiet shhh noise. "Don't tell everyone but he is absolutely correct and that's what happens behind the grey door at the end of the room. That's why we have bars on all the doors and windows otherwise everyone could get in to enjoy it." Timothy's mum tut tutted under her breath and looked at the ceiling. Uncle Fingers smiled and winked.

On the way home, Timothy asked his mum about granny's and great grandma's fortune telling skills, but his mum said she would not talk about such rubbish. So instead he played

Pig Chase on his mum's phone all the way home. His score was 128,753,297,000,245, which was an all-time high. Despite all the grey, Timothy had enjoyed his visit to prison.

Although Mum was always pleased to see Uncle Fingers, she also knew there was always a reason why Uncle Fingers visited. So, she wasn't surprised when, after a piece of Mint Wafer Cold Tea Sponge Cake and two cups of coffee, Uncle Fingers came out with his Next Great Idea.

Firstly, he tried to sell everyone packets of very cheap cigarettes, a couple of just released DVDs without covers, a Y-Box splashed with white paint, and some Crocodile sweatshirts that only had a small stain on the front. He had no takers. So, then he asked Timothy's mum if she would like to buy a new car. When Mum asked him what type of car he was selling, he replied, "What type of car do you want to buy?" Timothy's dad guffawed and murmured, "He'll be back inside before he knows it at this rate!"

Timothy's mum loved Uncle Fingers – he was her brother after all – and knew he needed the money so she bought the sweatshirts for Dad. She said he could use them when he was painting the house and doing the garden. Timothy had never seen his dad paint the house and they had a gardener who did the garden. However, Timothy heard his dad mutter, "Thanks for nothing!" under his breath as he accepted the sweatshirts from his brother-in-law.

Mum clapped her hands and said it had been lovely to see Uncle Fingers but he really should go so that he did not miss any good offers at the

Donkey and Daisy (his favourite pub around the corner).

Before Uncle Fingers left for the pub, Timothy agreed to meet him the next day and plan his revenge on the triplet bullies. Unfortunately, Uncle Fingers was detained by the fraud squad the next day, who wanted to interview him at length about a range of funny coloured bank notes he had used to buy a ham and mushroom pizza the previous week. Uncle Fingers maintained he knew nothing about any fraudulent behaviour and explained that he had just been practising colouring in the pretty pictures on the photocopy bank notes he had found and that they must have become mixed up in his wallet.

The bullies would never understand just how much they should thank the fraud squad for distracting Uncle Fingers just as he was about to take up their case when he was still very angry about it.

Lying in bed that night, Timothy dreamed of what would happen when he next saw Uncle Fingers, what would be his reaction, and would he make matters worse or could they be clever and find a way to stop the triplets from making his life and the life of many others so awful.

Chapter 10
Jaws 12 Horror Movie

Later that day, when Uncle Fingers was happily on his way to The Donkey and Daisy, Timothy's dad decided to organise a treat for the whole family so that his birthday would be a very special family day. This year's birthday treat was a trip to the cinema.

Mum was anxious and so pleaded with Dad to let her drive to the cinema. She struggled to cope with Dad's driving and she did not need the additional stress of him trying to park the car. Dad was not a bad driver; he was an awful driver. He did not concentrate, and this lack of focus was really dangerous when he was on busy roads. Timothy's dad always used his hands to express how he was feeling or to describe an event or something he had seen. This was fine when you were standing next to him in the safety of your front garden. However, it felt a lot less safe when Dad was hurtling down the road at 70 miles an hour. The car swayed from left to right and right to left. The worst part of his driving was that Dad did not notice he was swaying in the road. Timothy's mum would sometimes shout at him to be careful but his dad would usually ignore her. If Dad was feeling brave, he would point out that he was the only one who had not had an accident in 35 years of driving.

Timothy & the Triplets Three

That never went down well. Because, according to Timothy's mum, she had only ever scratched the door once when she got out of the car to fill up with petrol and hit the petrol pump bollard – however, she was never allowed to forget it.

Through gritted teeth, Timothy's mum would suggest he should look in the rear-view mirror. Behind him would be a scene of chaos as exasperated drivers screeched across the road as Dad danced his way to where he was going. He would be hopping from lane to lane at a moment's notice with little regard for other drivers and only an occasional random use of the indicators. Timothy's dad was right though, he had not been in an accident for 35 years, but he had caused multiple accidents to those drivers caught in his wake.

The children always thought it was quite fun being in the car when Dad was driving – a bit like being on a roller-coaster – and would laugh as they shouted "Scream if you wanna go faster!"

Dad loved Lulabella with all his heart but he never understood why she laughed at his driving because she had failed her Driving Theory Test for the 23rd time. Lulabella complained that the computer had it in for her, but no one listened. "Like father like daughter" was all Timothy's mum would have to say about that.

Even after Father Mike had blessed Dad's car and given him a St Jeremy pendant (the patron saint of bad drivers) to hang on the mirror, it didn't seem to make much difference. Although Dad could not see what all the fuss was about because, as he said, he always got home safely.

Eventually, Dad relented and agreed to let Mum drive to the cinema in her big, powerful Rover Ranger. Mum drew a huge sigh of relief.

Timothy & the Triplets Three

Arriving on time, they found a parking space and parked neatly with no problems. Dad was oblivious to how different this journey was compared to his last visit to cinema when he drove the family car, causing several accidents, lots of hand waving, a few hand gestures from other car drivers and two minor hearts attacks.

They went to the cinema to watch *Jaws 12* – it's the one where the children swim too far out to sea, a mutated shark circles the young children, they scream but the shark thrashes around in the water, getting ever closer to the hysterical children, who start to drown. Finally, the huge shark begins to eat them feet first.

As the children's blood spills into the water and as the screaming gets louder and louder, a pair of very tanned athletic lifeguards swim out to them. They fight off the shark and retrieve the children's feet from the shark's mouth, heroically rescuing the children, who are still screaming. The lifeguards, who are also models and romantically involved, swim several miles back to the beach with a child in one hand and the other hand holding the gory feet. It is not clear how the lifeguards are swimming because both their hands are full of footless children and gory feet – but nobody notices this because of the very loud music, the blood and screaming children.

The anxious parents of the children, who are also going through a difficult period in their relationship, are waiting to hug them at the shoreline. They cry endlessly whilst realising that they still love each other deeply.

As the music grows louder, the casualties are rushed to the emergency helicopter, which lands from nowhere on the beach, but miraculously does not blow sand into anyone's eyes. The helicopter pilot, Captain Dontflytoolow, who is also a WWE international wrestler, nods at the lifeguards and takes the screaming (footless) children to an emergency landing base on top of the Accident and Emergency hospital.

Once inside the hospital, the children are put on stretchers and wheeled at great speed down 362 corridors and into the operating theatre where the top foot surgeon, Dr Stitchitupquick (he is also staring as Detective Noclue in a New York police series about lost dogs), sews the screaming children's feet back on.

The children's feet are sewn back on successfully after 26 hours of non-stop surgery whilst the family exchange mid-distance stares across the waiting room and relive many

Timothy & the Triplets Three

memories of the children from happier times when they had feet. Well, successfully sewn back on is perhaps not the right phrase, because the children's feet were sewn back on, but they were sewn back on the wrong children. One child ended up with two left feet and the other child ended up with two right feet. This was great for the three-legged race, but not so good for ballroom dancing (of which the children were huge fans). The film ends when the children win *Strictly Come Dancing*.

When the lights came on in the movie theatre, Timothy noticed that they were sitting behind Arnold and Sylvia Fullofsnot, the parents of the bully triplets. Mrs Fullofsnot was 4 feet tall and Mr Fullofsnot was 6 foot 6 inches tall, so Timothy could only just see the top of Mrs Fullofsnot's head, even though she was sitting on a booster seat. Dad

Timothy & the Triplets Three

asked Mr and Mrs Fullofsnot if they had enjoyed *Jaws 12*. They both nodded that yes, indeed they had, but Mrs Fullofsnot added that all she had seen was a lot of sky because the seat in front of her was in the way. Timothy's dad nodded sympathetically then continued to speak his thoughts out loud, saying he thought the children in the movie were very lucky to escape with their lives, but it was unfortunate the hospital had sewn the wrong body parts on the wrong children. Timothy's dad then went on to contemplate aloud if this is what had happened to test tube children who seemed to have many of the wrong body parts in the wrong place or on the wrong child. Timothy's mum kicked his dad hard on the shins and quickly changed the subject.

Dad turned to Timothy and said, just loud enough so that his mum could almost hear, that

Timothy & the Triplets Three

Mr and Mrs Fullofsnot have a difficult marriage because they don't see eye to eye very often, but he bet that Mrs Fullofsnot never criticised Mr Fullofsnot's driving.

As the grown-ups continued to chat, Timothy wondered if Bert had been attacked by a shark and this was why he was still limping? He daydreamed that Bert had been able to swim back to shore with one foot missing, but his brothers Eddy and Neddy had been devoured slowly by a hungry shark. He dreamed of watching the Fullofsnots slowly, painfully getting guzzled by a shark in a frenzied attack. It would make so many people happy at his school.

As they left the cinema, Timothy's family were all in agreement that it was a good film, better than *Snatched 6*, which they had seen on

Dad's birthday the previous year. *Snatched 6* is a movie about a father who goes on holiday with his teenage daughter. She is snatched by a group of crazed European kidnappers. It is part of a series. At the end of *Snatched 1*, the daughter had been returned to her family and her dad is a hero because he has single-handedly fought off the 23 kidnappers and snatched his daughter out of the clutches of the bad guys. By the time *Snatched 6* was launched at cinemas, the daughter was sort of getting used to being kidnapped. The Dad was played by a different actor, and the daughter had acquired a few brothers and sisters who did not exist in *Snatched 1*. It also appeared she had become a black belt in several martial arts. Between the dad and the snatched daughter, they disposed of 67 kidnappers, avoided 6 near death experiences, dodged hundreds of bullets at close range, deactivated a nuclear bomb that was big enough to smash the galaxy into smithereens, and had been revived from certain death twice. On the way home, Dad had said he thought the movie was daft, but he particularly thought the dad in the movie was daft. Timothy asked why.

"Well, any father who allows his daughter to be snatched six times by kidnappers has something seriously wrong with him. One kidnapping is unlucky, but six kidnappings is totally irresponsible."

At the time, Timothy had asked where the Snatched family were next planning on going on holiday. He wondered if he could suggest the same spot to Mr and Mrs Fullofsnot. Then the triplets would be snatched and, because he knew nobody would ever pay a ransom to release them, that would be them gone for good. Timothy's dad

Timothy & the Triplets Three

laughed out loud and agreed. Mum just scowled and warned him he was on thin ice. Dad muttered under his breath that he wished the test tube triplets were on thin ice.

Chapter 11
Mad Dog Muncher Triumphs

A few days later, Timothy thought that Uncle Fingers had forgotten all about the bullying incident. However, that wasn't the case, and one day after tea, Timothy was lying on his bed listening to a new song by Miley Cyrus called 'Midnight Sky' when he heard a strange dog barking outside. At first he ignored it, but when it started to howl, he went to the window and saw Uncle Fingers with his hands around his mouth, just about to offer another yelp. Uncle Fingers beckoned Timothy downstairs.

Timothy & the Triplets Three

Uncle Fingers had hatched a devious plan – The Plan. That afternoon he would meet Timothy after school with Mad Dog Muncher and Crazy Chris Smasher. He had met both of these gentlemen in prison recently and, because they had so many shared interests, they had become good friends.

Mad Dog Muncher (his real name was Alan Smith) got his nickname because one day he was hungry but had no money. He knew of a restaurant that was offering free food for a year to anybody who could eat 100 'Mad Dogs' in an hour. Each Mad Dog was a 500 gram hot dog in a French bread roll, with mustard, tomato sauce, onions, squeezy cheese and hot, hot, hot chilli sauce. One hundred 'Mad Dogs' would be the equivalent of eating 525 iced doughnuts or 485 Quarter Pounder Cheeseburgers. Now this was a lot of hot dogs, and then to try to eat them in an hour would be an amazing feat. Twenty-six people had attempted the challenge, including a female wrestler from Halifax, a retired policeman from Coverack in Cornwall who could whistle Happy Birthday backwards in Spanish, and a kilt-wearing German speaking Welshman from Paris who was very confused.

Alan went along to the restaurant to stake his claim for the '100 Mad Dogs in an hour' challenge. The chef would prepare the Mad Dogs diligently, each one grilled to perfection, with lashings of sauces and onions. As the chef got towards 50 Mad Dogs in a challenge, he added more and more chilli sauce to burn the inside of the contestants' mouths. This always meant they failed the challenge and had to pay the £1,500 penalty fee. However, on this occasion, the chef had not calculated the impact it would have on the contestant if he did not have the money to pay the penalty. It simply meant that Alan could not afford to fail. By the time Alan was ready to start the challenge there was quite a crowd gathered to watch him fail, just like every contestant before him.

What they did not know was that Alan had a secret weapon; he had been born with four stomachs. Now some may consider this a disability, but Alan had always felt it was a huge asset. He was also born with webbed feet – again, some may consider this to be a disability, but Alan used this unusual feature to win all the swimming galas (his Aunty Maud was forever putting his name forward). He also had double-jointed shoulders, which was brilliant for slipping through iron bars when he needed to … escape (for whatever reason). The fact that one leg was shorter than the other was no problem for Alan because this meant he could hide up to £100,000 in cash in the shoe of his shortened leg and never limp during a getaway.

Alan made an energetic start by eating the first three Mad Dogs in one mouthful. The crowd who had been cheering fell silent and the only noise was a large gulp of air by the chef. Alan winked at his fans and consumed another three, and another three, and another three, and another three, and then to a standing ovation he stood on one leg and slid six Mad Dogs down in one go. The chef had his head in his hands, but he

Timothy & the Triplets Three

heard the loud cheers of encouragement as Alan consumed the first 50 Mad Dogs in less than 12 minutes. Alan then asked the chef for some more chilli sauce because he loved it so much. The chef was almost in tears. As Alan approached his 73rd Mad Dog in under 27 minutes, he stopped and offered the chef a deal. Alan announced he would be prepared to sign up to a double or quits deal. This meant he would try to eat 200 Mad Dogs in an hour, and this would win his friend free food for a year as well, but if he failed, he would win nothing. The chef happily agreed and immediately started to cook an additional 100 Mad Dogs. Alan got into his stride and the crowd clapped and cheered every time he slid a Mad Dog down his throat. Alan even threw a few into the air, swallowing them whole. He actually sucked one through a straw and he poured petrol over number 100, set it on fire, and ate it whilst the flames licked the bun (please do not try this at home!). The crowd was delirious. With only 17 minutes to go, he started on the second hundred Mad Dogs. The chef had managed to regain his composure. He was convinced that there was no way, no way on earth Alan could eat another 100 Mad Dogs in 17 minutes. His money was safe and Alan would have to hand over the cash and walk home a failure.

A few hours later, Alan was very pleased with himself. He had finished signing autographs and completed all his media interviews. The chef was still in tears. He could not believe what he had seen. Alan had eaten the last 100 Mad Dogs in batches of 10 at a time. He completed the task in less than 11 minutes and asked for a couple of banana sundaes because he still had some room

Timothy & the Triplets Three

in stomach number 3. This is how Alan got his nickname, Mad Dog Muncher.

Crazy Chris Smasher was actually called Chris Smasher. He got his nickname because he liked to say Crazy to most questions he was asked. For example:

You ok Chris?

Crazy...

How do you feel Chris?

Crazy...

What are you up to Chris?

Crazy...

What do you think of this party Chris?

Crazy...

How is the food Chris?

Crazy ...

Timothy & the Triplets Three

What is 2 + 2 Chris?

Crazy…

So, that is how Chris got the nickname Crazy Chris Smasher.

Uncle Fingers said The Plan was that when Timothy came out of school, he would make sure he was just in front of the bully triplets. Then Mad Dog Muncher and Crazy Chris Smasher would push into Timothy and he would turn around and tell Muncher and Smasher to watch where they were going, then poke them hard on the end of their crooked noses. Muncher and Smasher would then apologise, beg forgiveness and thank Timothy for not using his black belt Num-bety martial arts on them. All of it would have to happen in front of the bully triplets. Uncle Fingers was obviously very excited about The

Timothy & the Triplets Three

Plan because he kept cackling and rubbing his hands together.

Timothy thought long and hard about the idea and thanked Uncle Fingers. He promised that if the trouble didn't stop he would not delay in calling in Uncle Fingers, Muncher and Smasher. However, for now he felt he should try to deal with the problem himself. Uncle Fingers reluctantly agreed and said they would be acquiring some new cars the next day instead, so he was busy anyway.

Timothy went back inside to where his mum was in the kitchen cooking his favourite chicken tomato pasta. Timothy pulled up a stool and chatted to his lovely mum. While his mum smiled and brought Timothy up to date on her latest baking experiments, he felt so warm, protected and happy. But there was a dark cloud hanging over him. He could not get the thought of those horrific triplet bullies out of his head. Here he was, sat in his house, with his lovely mum knowing nothing and no one could save him from further misery. He desperately tried to think of the words to explain how these bullies controlled his life. But when his mum suddenly asked if he was ok, if something was worrying him, he muttered a denial. When she pushed again, asking the same question then saying, "Don't worry about anything, I have your back," he could feel his eyes filling up and so he shook his head and said he was going to have a shower.

Chapter 12
Living With a Saint

Timothy's mum was lovely, kind and warm, and the best mum in the world. She had blonde hair which was always tied back in an elastic band. She loved Timothy and he loved her right back. She also loved him brushing his teeth three times a day for eight minutes. She loved him only having half a glass of orange juice in the mornings to make sure his teeth did not rot. She loved him going to bed at 8.30pm without any fuss. She loved him eating five fruit and vegetables a day. She loved him never sticking cotton wool buds in his ears and she loved him polishing his shoes each night before school. In fairness, she loved him even when he did none of these things, but she hoped one day he would start doing them all.

Everyone would tell Timothy "your mum is lovely and kind". Father Mike once suggested that Timothy's mum was so kind that they should have a cash collection and commission a stained-glass window for the church. Timothy's dad spluttered at this and said it wasn't always easy living with a saint. He wondered quietly to himself if they would think his wife was a saint if they knew she rarely put the top back on the toothpaste, never put the bins out on a Thursday, sang the wrong words to songs all the time, and sometimes used a teabag twice.

Despite all this, Timothy's mum was lovely and kind. She was kind to the lady across the street who lost her cat all the time and she never complained when she was asked to pick up her friends' children from school.

His mum could be found most days helping in school. She was the Chair of the Parent Teacher Association (PTA). This meant she organised the fundraising for the school by holding Summer fairs, Christmas fairs, Autumn fairs, Easter Fairs, Winter Fairs, Spring Fairs, Halloween Fairs, Bonfire Night Fairs and sometimes, if she ran out of ideas (which wasn't very often), she just held Fairs.

Timothy & the Triplets Three

Timothy's house was full of boxes with the remnants of past fairs, as well as boxes that were full of the contents of future fairs. The boxes could contain: raffle prizes (past and future), rejected second-hand toys, leaflets, flyers, fancy dress costumes, banners, a roll of paper tablecloth, teabags, sticky tape, bunting (Timothy wondered where bunting got its name 'bunting' from? There wasn't a bun to be seen!), crayons, walkie-talkie radios (without batteries), printed T-shirts, chocolate, bags of old pennies, rubber gloves, washing up liquid, clothes, marker pens (dried up with no lids), thick white card, emergency toilet roll, first aid kit, random mobile phone chargers, glitter and thank you letters. You name it, it would be in one of the boxes

Over the years, his mum recycled raffle prizes. She would buy raffle tickets from anybody and everybody to support them and their cause. This included the Scouts, the Lifeboat Institution, the Blind Bat Association, and the Weeding Society. When she won prizes, she would put them in her raffle recycling box so they could be raffled at one of her many fairs in the future. Sometimes raffle prizes would be recycled three or four times before a lucky winner would keep them. One of his mum's famous prizes was a set of three multi-coloured plastic poop scoops – only used a few times. But nobody minded as everyone loved Timothy's mum.

As well as boxes full of recycled raffle prizes, Timothy's mum had two garden sheds full of the big equipment you needed to hold fairs. There was a Pluck-a-Duck inflatable swimming pool with 39 yellow plastic ducks. There should have been 40 ducks, but next door's dog had somehow got hold of number 23 and refused to bring it back. There was a Coconut Shy. Timothy always wondered why it was called a Coconut Shy. He could understand the coconut bit, but why was it shy? Perhaps it had become embarrassed at the rust on the coconut holders? Or perhaps it had just always been shy?

There were two bouncy castles; one had a small hole in it that his dad was supposed to fix, so even when it was fully blown up, it was not really bouncy. Timothy had suggested they rename it the Floppy Castle, but his mum scowled and said no. There were candyfloss machines, tea urns, cooking pots, plastic plates, cups and glasses. In one corner was a Roll-a-Penny stall that now had to be changed to 'Roll-a-10p'. "Bloomin' inflation," his dad had muttered when Timothy's mum had asked him to change it.

Timothy & the Triplets Three

Timothy was confused: how could it be inflation? The Floppy Castle needed inflation, not the Roll-the-10p stall.

Timothy's favourite was Bash-a-Rat. The poor raggedy rats looked very sorry for themselves as they slid down the drainpipe, waiting for some excited child to whack them again and again and again.

The Wire Buzzer was broken after Dad got so excited when he managed to complete it after about 47 attempts. He wasn't given a prize because the lady from church who was running the buzzer stall said the battery was worn out, and anyway, the prizes were really for children not parents. Dad sulked for hours after that.

Soak a Teacher was a favourite at school, as long as you could get the most hated teachers to put their heads in the hole whilst children threw

Timothy & the Triplets Three

wet sponges at them. Mr Slippity-Dippity, the French teacher, always attracted lots of customers as long as you could get him to stay in long enough. The children at Timothy's school would rather eat their own toenails than learn French from Mr Slippity-Dippity. The problem was that Mr Slippity-Dippity had a very strong Russian accent which made understanding him in English hard enough but trying to understand his Russian/French was really hard. But there was more: Mr Slippity-Dippity loved garlic; he had garlic on his cornflakes, he had garlic on his sandwiches and he even drank hot cups of garlic in the staff room. His love of garlic went so far that even his fellow teachers kept their distance. Mr Slippity-Dippity stank of garlic morning, noon and night.

Mr Tiddles (if truth be known was not really a proper teacher, but he liked to hang out with

Timothy & the Triplets Three

the teachers in the staff room because he thought it made him look cool) was the educational peer reviewer for forms 3,4, 5c, 6a+f, 8a and 15. This was really strange, because no one who hung out with the teachers looked cool and the school did not have a class 6f and 15. It was clear that Mr Tiddles lived in a fantasy world and so he was dragged into the Soak a Teacher stall one year to see if they could wake him up from his fantasy world. The more he protested, the more everyone cheered and jeered to get him to stick his head in the soaking hole. The first sponge missed him completely; the second sponge caught his cheek and nose with a great big splash. However, it was the third sponge which proved deadly and most memorable. It knocked off Mr Tiddles' toupee, much to the gasps of everyone who was watching. Mum said the money raised when Mr Tiddles

Timothy & the Triplets Three

stayed in the teacher soaker all afternoon beat every other stall because there was such a huge queue to soak him.

Timothy loved playing in the sheds and improving his skills for the next fair his mum was organising. After a few years, Mum had to retire him from playing the games because he had mastered the skills needed for each one and won more prizes than anyone else.

When Timothy's mum was not helping others, running the PTA or leading a multitude of fairs, she was coming up with new ideas. She had ideas for everything. She never ran out of ideas. She dreamt of ideas, shared ideas, sketched ideas and even had ideas about ideas. She had one book full of ideas. Some ideas were scribbled on the back of till receipts; other ideas were written on her hand. One day, Timothy feared the worst when she was having difficulty remembering one of her ideas and said, "Hang on a minute, it's on the tip of my tongue." He was concerned that she would open her mouth and he would see more ideas written there!

The most important thing was that Timothy's mum was lovely and kind, and she loved Timothy. And Timothy loved her back.

Even though Timothy loved his mum and he knew she loved him right back, he could not tell her about the bully triplets. He knew she would be upset, maybe she would not believe the three darling triplets could be so grotesque and mean. She was forever sticking up for them when his dad said something bad about them. On the other hand, he was worried she would try to sort it out

Timothy & the Triplets Three

by inviting the triplets to their house for tea. He knew that, because his mum was so lovely, she would not be able to understand how horrid some people can be to others. So, he just kept quiet, hoping that one day a solution would appear and the nightmare would end.

Chapter 13
The Amazing Lulabella

Of course, although Timothy knew his mum loved him, he had a tough act to follow because his big sister was amazing. Everyone kept telling Timothy that Lulabella was amazing – including her. "I am amazing, Timothy, simply amazing!" Timothy agreed that his sister was amazing and told everybody. "My sister tells me she is amazing, she tells me every day."

His sister was 18 years old and amazing. She had attended the same school as Timothy and so all his teachers knew of him before he arrived. "How is Lulabella?" they would ask, usually followed by saying, "Your big sister is amazing!"

Timothy was not sure why she was amazing; he just knew she was. Maybe Lulabella was amazing because she baked the best lemon drizzle cakes in the universe. Perhaps she was amazing because she was in the London 2012 Olympics opening ceremony as a dancer. For weeks beforehand, she would practise her routine in front of the mirror. Timothy learnt the dance as well, and watching her twirl and glide 100 times a day was intoxicating. Or maybe, as Dad suggested, she was amazing because she managed to create the world's toughest obstacle course in her bedroom by throwing all her clothes on the floor in such a way it was impossible not to fall over when trying to wake her up in the morning.

Timothy & the Triplets Three

Sadly for Timothy, Lulabella had recently started a year at university in America, where she was being amazing. The house felt utterly empty without her in it. There was no one arguing about the bathroom, no one cluttering the bathroom with all sorts of make-up and no one eating the last chocolate teddy bear biscuit that Timothy had hidden behind the pile of tins of herrings in the cupboard.

But Timothy was looking forward to Christmas because Lulabella was coming home for the holidays so that she could remind the whole family how amazing she was. Timothy loved Lulabella coming home from America because she always brought him gifts: the newest Spikey trainers in black; a signed basketball from Lkistsb Dheutres (or Timothy thought that was what it said), apparently the best basketball player in the NFL; and gobstoppers from The World Famous Florida Gobstoppers Emporium. (They were huge and came with a guarantee to 'stop anybody's gob'. Timothy made a claim against the guarantee because he asked Nan to test suck the gobstoppers and she sucked three gobstoppers at once and carried on complaining about the weather.)

Although Timothy managed to speak with Lulabella often on FaceTime, it wasn't the same as having her around. He wanted to tell Lulabella about the bullies because she had been bullied at school, but he wasn't sure he would be able to confide in her about his problems.

When Lulabella started at secondary school, a girl had picked on her, calling her names, hiding her books, pushing her around, sticking 'kick me' signs on her back and making her miserable.

After a few weeks, her class went on a nature trip to a local park. They had to work in pairs to spot all the different trees and write them down. At lunchtime, the bully stole Lulabella's nature book containing all her notes and refused to give it back. Then she stole her drink and poured it over the grass. Finally, she grabbed Lulabella's cheese sandwich – but this is where she became unstuck. The bully walked over to the lake and, in front of all the class, broke off pieces of Lulabella's cheese sandwich and fed it to the ducks. What happened next caused everyone (including the teachers) to stand up and watch in horror and delight. As the ducks rushed over to grab some of the sandwich, it started a duck feeding frenzy. The bully had over 50 ducks squawking, flapping their wings, snapping their beaks and trying to grab some of the sandwich. The bully panicked and screamed, trying to run away, but the ducks followed her, lunging to grab a piece of cheese sandwich. Lulabella clapped her hands in delight as the bully tripped over and fell into the lake, headfirst.

When she emerged like a bog monster from the deep, she was covered in mud, duck feathers and weeds. Her hair was drenched with the stagnant water from the lake. Everybody (including the teachers, the teaching assistants and the parent helpers) was laughing until they had tears in their eyes. The bully tried to climb out of the lake but slipped back in several times until eventually she was pulled out by some teachers. She looked like a muddy scarecrow and smelt so bad that she had to sit on bin bags on the bus back to school so she did not damage the seats. She had to sit near the teachers in the front of the bus while the rest of the class tried to sit as far back in the bus as they could to get away from the stench.

The bully's parents both worked, so she had to wait in the after-school club dressed in clothes from the lost property department. She wore one yellow football sock, one dirty blue hockey sock, boy's school shorts, a pirate T-shirt and ballet shoes.

After the incident, whenever Lulabella would see her in school, she would ask the bully if she would like some more of her sandwiches and everybody would laugh. The bully never bothered Lulabella again.

Timothy hoped and hoped that one day the bully triplets would fall foul in a similar way. With Lulabella in the USA, he would just have to sort his problems out alone.

Chapter 14
Timothy's Christmas list

Timothy loved Christmas. He loved Christmas because everyone was happy, there was snow, great Christmas tunes, tasty food (and lots of it), happy ending movies and lots of family time.

However, after writing his letter to Father Christmas for the 23rd time, he was still unhappy with his choices:

- ✓ Glitter Super Mango Slider Scooter with whizz sound effects

Timothy & the Triplets Three

- ✓ Life size Mudflips singing Ratnatz (version 2)
- ✓ Sweets with popping hopping candy
- ✓ Chocolate spiders (real spiders covered in chocolate)
- ✓ Two large sets of anti-snoring restraints for Dad
- ✓ Earplugs for the whole family in case the anti-snoring kits didn't work
- ✓ Toiletries for Mum so she could raffle them later in the year at the school fair
- ✓ Water pistol with laser aiming device (look out neighbours)
- ✓ Lego Buckingham Palace with real LED chandeliers
- ✓ Hoola Hoops for Nan and a shaving kit for her moustache
- ✓ Hollywood style photo shoot for Lulabella

Timothy & the Triplets Three

- ✓ Two turtles, a penguin and a giraffe
- ✓ Endless chicken fajitas and baked beans
- ✓ CCTV for the lunatic next door so that Timothy could record his antics and sell them to *You Have Been Framed*
- ✓ A 1958 Eldorado Cadillac 6 litre V 8

But even with the penguins added at the last minute, he felt it was missing something, something different, something unique, something from the end of the world or, even better, from another world. He thought and thought about it. He could not sleep. He walked aimlessly around the house seeking inspiration.

Eventually, he went into the garden and climbed onto the huge trampoline he had received for his last birthday and lay back, staring at the sky. Looking up at the stars and

Timothy & the Triplets Three

dreaming of how they were made gave him an idea in a flash. Well, not a flash of light, but a flash of brilliance. He had seen a TV advert for an electrical device that emitted a high pitch noise that could only be heard by animals. It was guaranteed to scare away unwanted cats and dogs from the garden. He had noticed there was a warning on the box that the device could play havoc with people's hearing aids. This was too good an opportunity to miss. He had observed recently that Eddy had started wearing a tiny hearing aid. No-one knew because he would cover it with his hair. But during one of their nasty episodes, when they rubbed Mr Yeastly's cake in Timothy's hair, Timothy had tried to push them away. As he did, Eddy stumbled and his hair moved, revealing the little silver piece in his ear. He quickly covered it, thinking

Timothy & the Triplets Three

Timothy had not noticed, but he had. He knew what it was straight away.

Could this be his chance to ward them off? If he asked for 10 of them and switched them on together, would they make enough noise to keep the bullies away from him? The triplets always worked as a pack of three, never on their own, so Timothy was sure that if he could keep one of them away, the remaining two would not bother him.

So it was settled. He would ask Father Christmas for 10 Super Sonic Electrical High-Pitched Animal Deterrent Alarms. The list was revised, and a merry Christmas assured for all.

Chapter 15
Christmas Mashup

It was only six weeks until Christmas and before then there was much that Timothy had to do, not least the school Christmas nativity play. Timothy had always enjoyed the school nativity play, even when he was the back end of the third camel for two years in a row. Many children would have been put off by the experience if they had slipped noisily off the stage during the birth of Jesus as he did in the first year, but Timothy had been unperturbed. Instead,

Timothy & the Triplets Three

Timothy saw it as an opportunity to create a headline – "Schoolboy injured as backend of camel slips off stage". (The Green Town Gazette loved his idea and used it on their front page.) A wise man and a shepherd with first aid skills saved him, thankfully. At the later performance, he was paraded down the centre of the audience (avoiding the stage altogether), which everyone agreed was a much grander entrance. Well, it would have been a grander entrance had it not been for Mrs Snuckle's walking stick tripping up the front half of the camel, containing a small boy from the year below Timothy called Henry Clunk, causing the camel to stumble. However, it was decided (inside the camel) that it would be better to slump in the aisle as though in awe of the nativity scene, rather than attempt a remount. The remainder of

Timothy & the Triplets Three

the nativity was conducted solemnly – apart from the constant giggles from within the slumped camel in the aisle. As always, Father Mike was unfazed; he had seen it all before and rather enjoyed the hilarity it brought to the annual performance.

This year, Timothy's schoolteacher, a rather young and inexperienced Mr Himalaya, decided to let the children write their own play and perform it at the end of term. Rather than stifle the children's creativity and innovation, he said that they could write and produce it themselves whilst he kept his headphones on and caught up on his friends' activities on TwoFacedbook.

Timothy & the Triplets Three

Mr Himalya was only just out of school himself and was the youngest teacher at the school. He always wore a white shirt, black pants (which were too short) and white sports socks which peeped out between his pant leg and his Tilby Trainers. Timothy thought Mr Himalya bought shirts which were two sizes too small so that it looked like he was always in the gym building his body. Unfortunately, the tight shirts did little to highlight his pectoral muscles, but they did shine a light on his developing beer belly.

Timothy and his friends thought this idea of giving them free rein was rather decent and so repaid his trust by promising to deliver a production that would live in the memories of all who saw it for many years. It was entitled 'Christmas Mashup'. Basically, it featured a rapper style musical score with words by pupils

Billy Vile, Susie Sour and Jason X. (After they left school, they went on to form the Three Angels Choral Rock group)

A cast of hundreds practised for days, re-enacting scenes from the battle of Hastings (a key plot twist), which ended with all cast members getting an arrow in the eye. Just when all seemed bleak Deliveroo turned up and delivered pizzas for everybody which put a smile on the whole cast face and restored everybody's eyesight.

On the night, Father Mike loved it so much that he led the chorus with Susie Vile. Apart from a few parents who wept, Lucy Giblets (who threw up over her grandad), and three mums who fainted at the arrow scene, everyone went home happy. (Although the whole cast did receive a thunderous telling off from Mrs Giswellian, the headteacher, at assembly the next day. Timothy's

Timothy & the Triplets Three

dad suggested Mr Himalaya would probably not return in the New Year – he was right.)

Mrs Giswellian was 52 years old. She smelt of old hamsters because, apparently, she used to breed them with her husband before he ran off with a rabbit breeder from a feeder primary school. Teachers always mentioned 'the feeder school', which worried all the primary school children because they thought when you went to high school you were getting 'fed' to something!

Since Mrs Giswellian's husband had left, she had a small fridge installed in her office which was full of Jim and Jack's Cookie Dough ice cream. On bad days, she could eat four full-size tubs. This might seem unhealthy, but at least it stopped her biting through her bottom lip with nerves – which she did most days. She wore down one of her front teeth biting her bottom lip, and the replacement false tooth was an odd brownish colour which matched her brownish hair and her brownish shoes. It was said that when she was younger, she had been a promising tap dancer until one day she fell in the kitchen sink and it brought her less than glittering career to an end.

Chapter 16
Mrs Ritkiks sings

The final countdown to Christmas had begun. Fake snow was strewn all over the place like Father Mike's dandruff, and Christmas carols were everywhere (except in church, where Father Mike was focusing on Grime music).

The season of goodwill was certainly creeping into the town, but there were areas where the goodwill was struggling to be heard because of the noisy new dog at number 26. Mrs Ritkiks, who lived at number 27 on Timothy's road and

Timothy & the Triplets Three

was the longest living resident in the street, was very upset. Not only was the new dog noisy but she was convinced it had eaten Lucile (her cat). Mrs Ritkiks said Lucile had never gone missing before and she had definitely never missed Lemon Meringue Pie, which was always the dessert on Tuesday. Mum was upset for Mrs Ritkiks and made a poster to be put up on the local streetlights. Mum also offered a reward if Lucile was found. Dad offered a reward if Lucile was not found. Dad was pleased Lucile was missing, as he had been trying to keep Lucile away with Tarmite Bon Bons for years. It wasn't that he hated all cats, but he drew the line at Lucile's constant piddling on his prize rhubarb. He even tried to wash Lucile's piddle off the rhubarb in the washing machine, but you could still taste Lucile's piddle in Mum's rhubarb crumble pie. (Nan complained because she said she preferred Lucile's piddle flavour to the taste of Dad's rhubarb.)

Timothy's dad secretly liked Mrs Ritkiks – not that he would ever admit it. She sang out of tune and very loudly in the bath most evenings. She bought an annual season ticket for the local buses so she could travel anywhere and everywhere whenever the fancy took her. She always wore hand-knitted cardigans and had lots of little plastic gnomes in her front garden. They wore a constant smile as they fished 365 days a year. Every window in her house had a plastic window box slung underneath it which was filled with dead flowers from the previous year. When the flowers were alive, they gave everybody a feel-good factor. However, Timothy's dad enjoyed them more when they were all dead. He liked Mrs

Ritkiks because it made him chuckle whenever he walked past her house in the evenings, admiring the dead flowers in her window box and listening to the out-of-tune songs coming from her bathroom window.

Timothy was convinced that Lucile had simply gone on holiday to Number 71, where Mr Yeastly was known to be testing out food for his latest attempt to win *I'm a Cook, Bake Me Out of Here*. Last year, he came a close second-to-last due to his sausage soufflé exploding live on TV. It was a real sensation, and even though there was a huge petition signed by all members of the Bangers and Mash Society (six people in total), he left the show after only two weeks. Lucile was known to be appreciative of his cooking and Timothy was sure she was just voting with her paws. If the truth be known, Lucile didn't much like Lemon

Meringue pie and only ate it to please poor Mrs Ritkiks.

In fact, Lucile had run away with the love of her life, Tom, a cat originally from Liverpool. They met once at the vets and it was a love affair which was written in the stars. After many years of planning, Tom and Lucile met at the end of the road and hitchhiked a lift on a fish lorry heading to the Liverpool docks. Once at the docks, they rendezvoused with a catamaran leaving for the Caribbean the next day. And so, they sailed off into the sunset and lived happily ever after, sailing the sun-soaked seas.

Chapter 17
Half a Christmas tree

At home, everybody was excited because Lulabella was due home from America. She would soon be reminding everyone of how amazing she was. Timothy's mum had decorated her room with stars and stripes, Christmas decorations and a beautiful fresh tree. Timothy had made an enormous wreath with oranges and holly. Her dad recorded a special selection of him singing her favourite Christmas carols at twice the normal speed.

Timothy & the Triplets Three

At 8pm Timothy and Mum were about to set off in the car to go to the airport to collect Lulabella, but Dad was unfortunately locked in the toilet. Mum asked if he had gone in there with his iPad. When Timothy confirmed he had entered the toilet with his iPad, she sighed and ran back inside. She shouted through the door that they needed to leave immediately and Dad shouted back that he would be finished on the loo once he had completed level 26 of Panda Chase (which was his favourite game). Timothy was not sure what his mum said but Dad was soon in the car with a twinkle in his eye. Mum was very quiet.

Timothy was excited at the thought of picking up Lulabella. He was so excited he had decided to put on a Santa outfit to greet her in airport arrivals and make her smile. She did smile when she saw him; in fact, everybody who saw him smiled.

Lulabella approached them with her eight suitcases and designer Chunnel bags. She was shouting, "Timothy, Timothy, Timothy, get my bags, get me a latté, hold my coat, I am so amazing, get me a Goodbye magazine, where is the car? Daddy, bring the car round!" – all without taking a breath!

Timothy was so happy. The Amazing Lulabella was home and all was well.

There was a sense of excitement and constant activity in the house in the run up to Christmas. Dad was nowhere he should have been (according to Mum), Lulabella was wrapping lots of nice treats and making homemade potpourri, and Timothy was so excited he could not sleep.

Christmas was not Christmas unless there was a ridiculously huge tree in the house. Timothy's

Timothy & the Triplets Three

family – Mum, Dad, Lulabella, Uncle Tony, Uncle George, his cousins and himself – were going to the local forest to choose and buy their Christmas tree. They were meeting their cousins there so they could all race around trying to find the best tree.

Lulabella rejected the first 738 Christmas trees as they were: not tall enough, not round enough, not smelly enough, not expensive enough or not glamorous enough. After much debate, a 15-foot tree was selected. It was wonderful: tall, triangular, green, fresh and very Christmassy.

However, it did not look quite so Christmassy once Dad had cut off the top 7 foot so that it would fit inside the house. This was done while Timothy's mum had popped round to Mrs Ritkiks' to offer her some mince pies.

Timothy & the Triplets Three

Nevertheless, once if had been positioned in the lounge and adorned with 17 boxes of lights, Christmas decorations and chocolate treats, it looked incredible – even though, as Lulabella said, it resembled an illuminated Benchers Brook Fence from the Grand National. Dad hated switching the lights on because every single year one or two sets of lights would not work. Although he tested the lights each year before he put them back in the box at the end of the season – and once again when he took them out the next year before he put them on the tree – once they were wrapped intricately around every branch, the lights would refuse to glimmer. This year, he had gone out and bought all new lights, and when no one was looking, he threw out the old ones. So, when he switched on the lights, he was triumphant. They shone like Blackpool illuminations. Dad said they were so bright they could be seen from space. Timothy and Lulabella giggled and shook their heads. Dad was cautiously optimistic that once Timothy's mum saw the Christmas tree she would be delighted. He was very wrong. Timothy's mum preferred the top half of the tree, the half he had chopped off, and so three days later when his dad was at work, his mum removed the bottom of the tree from the house and replaced it with the top section then redecorated it from top to bottom. Worse still, his dad never noticed.

Timothy's dad was usually wrong about most things; he had this nasty habit of just being wrong. Timothy's mum suggested he should go to the doctor and see if he needed any tablets or medicine. Lulabella said it was ok for Dad to be wrong about everything because he was old, a man, and Dad.

Timothy would just smile and nod knowingly when his dad said yet another wrong thing.

Timothy & the Triplets Three

Timothy was convinced that most of the times his dad was wrong just to make everyone laugh – but, in fact, often he was just wrong.

Dad said that when he was younger, he was always right, but since he had been married, he was mostly wrong about mostly everything.

There were some famous examples of Dad being wrong: when he caught the train to Skegness and woke up in Penzance, or when he put salt on his chips only to find it was sugar, or when he put his boxer shorts on back to front and could not go to the loo all day, or when he said he was a good driver. Mum would despair, Lulabella would tut and look at the ceiling whilst smiling, and Timothy would giggle and wink at his dad. Timothy never quite understood what Lulabella and Mum were looking at when they looked at the ceiling, but he knew it must be important because it always made them both tut and shake their heads.

However, when it truly mattered, Timothy's dad was mostly right.

It was the same with his dad's deafness; it sort of came and went of its own accord. Mum suggested he went to the doctors or get a hearing aid. Dad would just say, "Pardon" and wink at Timothy. Timothy noticed his dad's hearing was always worse when he was being given instructions about shopping, cleaning or going to visit relatives.

Once, Dad did not hear Timothy's mum tell him to pick up Nan on Christmas Eve on the way back from Sainsbury's. When he came back, he had remembered the batteries for the remote-controlled dinosaurs, whipping cream for Mum's toxic sherry trifle, earplugs for when cousin Julie

Timothy & the Triplets Three

sang Christmas carols, drawing pins for the 'Pin the Crown on The Three Wise Men' game after lunch, and a box of half-priced Christmas cards for all the people Mum forgot to send cards to that year. The trip was a great success in Dad's mind. However, the trip was a disaster, thought Mum, who wanted to know where Nan was.

Dad said it was easy to forget something; it was just unfortunate it was the fourth time he had forgotten to pick Nan up (that week). Mum was fuming and gave him 'the look'. Timothy's mum was lovely and kind, but if you crossed the line you would get 'the look'. Mum never understood what 'the look' was, but everyone who had been given 'the look' knew exactly what 'the look' was.

Dad was given 'the look' more than anybody, closely followed by Lulabella, who pretended she did not see 'the look'. But Timothy knew that

Lulabella did see 'the look' because she would always retreat upstairs into her obstacle course bedroom and lay low for a while.

Even though he had been given 'the look', Dad chuckled, took his life in his own hands by pinching Mum's cheek, and set off back to the car to pick up Nan.

Lulabella always stuck up for Dad, even though he was usually wrong. She said that she worried about his self-esteem if nobody stuck up for him, and she always took his meals out to the kennel when he was in the bad books. Timothy had taken this role on for Dad when Lulabella went to university. It was great that Lulabella was back for a bit to take on the role again.

Chapter 18
Grotesque triplet bullies

Timothy loved Christmas shopping. It was magical to go into town and buy special gifts for his mum, dad and sister. The lamp posts all had twinkly lights strewn between them, the shop windows were decorated beautifully, the pastries had cinnamon inside, and everybody was singing Christmas carols. He had taken £30 of his hard-earned cash from his piggy bank and it was crammed in his pocket, soaked with the moisture from his excited sweaty hand.

Timothy & the Triplets Three

As he headed off to the bus stop just around the corner from his house, he heard the dreaded but familiar shouting of the bully boy triplets. He sighed. Timothy had been looking forward to this trip for weeks and he did not want to bump into the bullying morons and let them spoil his magical day. But as Timothy tried to hide by pushing himself into a big hedge by the bus stop, the bullies came around the corner and spotted his trainers sticking out of the bottom of the leafless bush. Timothy's heart sank as he heard their footsteps grind to a halt and Eddy say, "What have we here?"

Eddy dragged him out of the hedge, then pushed him back in again whilst accompanied by Neddy's laughter, soon replaced with him singing the hokey cokey. Repeatedly, Eddy pushed Timothy in, out, in, out, shaking him all about in the hedge.

Timothy & the Triplets Three

Finally, when Eddy's arms had tired, Timothy was allowed out of the hedge, scratched, dirty, covered in cobwebs and looking like a scarecrow, with his hair stood at right angles to his head. Neddy and Eddy stood there laughing at him, and Timothy's heart sank to his boots in fear and shame. He turned to see what Bert was doing but noticed it was just the two of them – Neddy and Eddy. There was no sign of Bert.

Timothy hoped they had had their fun with him. Sadly, the torment was only just starting. They took it in turns to spit in his hair until it looked like he had just come out of the shower. Neddy and Eddy kicked Timothy until he cried.

Luckily, the bus arrived, prompting the triplets to stop their bullying. However, as they turned to leave, Neddy saw Timothy reach into his pocket for his bus fare. As soon as Neddy saw the £30,

Timothy & the Triplets Three

he snatched it and, in a second, the triplets were gone. The bus stopped, the doors opened, and Timothy knelt on the pavement, drenched in Eddy and Neddy's spit, covered in hedge cobwebs, battered and kicked, with tears rolling down his cheeks. The kind bus driver asked him if he was ok. Timothy smiled, nodded slowly and walked away from the bus towards the park, where he was able to sit down and collect his thoughts for a few hours before returning home, giftless and so very sad.

When he tried to creep silently up the stairs, Timothy's dad called from the living room to ask if he had enjoyed his Christmas shopping and got what he wanted. Timothy put his head around the door, gave him his best smile, shrugged his dirty shoulders and said, "Yes, thanks Dad. I will most probably pop into town next week with Nan and finish off my shopping."

Timothy was usually a happy boy; he had a great family and lots of fun friends. But the misery he felt in lying to his dad, pretending nothing had happened, and realising that his life would never be any different, made his soul plummet to the end of the world. These moments made him feel so dark and helpless. He sat in his room, alone, bewildered and cried quietly. Why could he not stick up for himself? Timothy knew the triplets would happily bash him every time they saw him, but they would never attack him if he was with Nan because she would hit them so hard with the walking stick, they would all limp for weeks.

He desperately wanted to share the constant fear he felt about the bullies with his dad, but he just could not get the words out. His dad was an amazing dad, but what could his dad do to stop the bullying? He would try to find the positive and look for the silver lining, as he always did. Maybe he would even try to joke about it to cheer Timothy up? Perhaps he would say, "Oh, don't worry Timothy, we all get bullied at school, it will pass." Or even worse, his dad would march around to the Fullofsnots' house and ask them politely to stop bullying his son. That would just make matters worse. He loved his dad, but he knew his dad would not be able to do anything to help tackle the bullies. There was nothing his dad could do to make it better, so why upset him by telling him how sad he was?

When there were no more tears, Timothy started to wonder why it was only Eddy and Neddy who had attacked him at the bus stop.

Timothy & the Triplets Three

The triplets always hunted in threes, but today there was no Bert. Surely he was not still limping after his crash with Stevo? Maybe the aliens had zapped him up and taken him to a faraway planet, mistaking him for one of their kind? Maybe he had fallen down a huge crevice which had opened up in front of his house after a very small and silent earthquake? Maybe a tiger in the local zoo had eaten him? He hoped that, whatever had happened to him, Bert had given up his addiction to making his life a misery. Perhaps dealing with only two of the triplets may be a little easier – then again, probably not.

Chapter 19
Fantastic 'Around the World' Advent Calendar

It was the first day of December and Timothy couldn't wait to open the first door in his advent calendar. His excitement about Christmas was building and, each year, starting the advent calendar made it all seem a bit more real. Each morning he would rush downstairs to open another day and reveal the gift behind the cardboard tab. Last year, Mum had bought Timothy a Lego advent calendar with a small

Timothy & the Triplets Three

Lego figure behind each door. The year before, it was chocolate snowman figures. This year, Dad had picked up a 'Smells From Around the World' advent calendar" off Dbay, the online shopping website. When he gave it to Timothy with a wide smile, Mum gave Dad 'the look'. Dad said it would be fine and very educational.

Timothy excitedly opened the first tab to reveal a small piece of card with a scratch and sniff arrow pointing to the centre. Timothy scratched and sniffed, watched from a distance by Mum and Dad. Soon everybody was running for the fresh air in the garden. Even Timothy was left gasping for breath. The stench was grim, just awful. It even made the new dog at number 26 stop howling as he gasped for fresh air too. Timothy turned over the piece of card to discover that the smell was described as 'A hint of the

Timothy & the Triplets Three

River Nile'. Mum decided there and then that she never ever wanted to venture to the River Nile. Dad and Timothy were inclined to agree.

Over the next few days, Timothy scratched and sniffed 'The Old Socks of a New Zealand Rugby Legend', 'Essence of Last Year's British Blue Cheese', 'Pure Brazilian Swamp', 'Rotten Chinese

Timothy & the Triplets Three

Eggs', and 'New York Teenager Bedroom' – which Timothy thought was quite normal and reminded him of Lulabella's bedroom. Timothy's favourite, 'Aunty's Early Morning Breath', brought back happy memories of Aunty Gloria just before she had all her teeth taken out. Timothy and his dad thought the advent calendar was a great success. Mum thought... well, actually, I can't tell you exactly what Mum thought because she always muttered it under her breath whilst shaking her head. Timothy looked at the website where they sold the advent calendar. They also sold one called '24 Unique Scents from Animal Bottoms from Around the World'. Timothy wondered if he could send one of those advent calendars to the Fullofsnots. He was sure they were animal lovers.

After the excitement of the advent calendar each morning, Timothy would walk to school, usually arriving late to ensure he was able to sell off his stock of out-of-date chocolate to the school bullies along the way. (They always thought they were far too cool to be on time for school, never mind – shock, horror – being early!) This day was no different.

As always, Timothy was looking for a new opportunity, a new product or service he could launch. He wanted to achieve his objective of becoming a teenage millionaire and could see no reason why he couldn't achieve this whilst giving the bullies a taste of their own medicine.

In the past, he had thought of selling watches because Uncle Fingers was always offering him a supply. However, after the sale of his first Colex watch went badly wrong when the English teacher he sold it to, Miss Honestly-Honest, had taken it to a local shop for repair and it turned out to be part of a stolen stash of Colex watches from Lord Dribbledownmychin, Timothy decided to leave watch sales to Uncle Fingers and his mates, the twins Tick and Tock.

Uncle Fingers had also offered him '750 very good quality and low cost 100-inch plasma TVs'. There was only a slight drawback – no plug or picture. Also, the remote controls were for a different brand of TV.

Once, he supplied Timothy with boxer shorts (which Timothy improved with itching powder). This gave Timothy the best laugh he had in ages. Just watching Frog Face, one of the local bully boys, dancing across the playground with his hands down his pants; it cheered Timothy up for weeks. Then there was the latest Tanyo Game Girl (without controls) and a selection of Chunnel designer handbags (with dodgy handles).

Timothy & the Triplets Three

Timothy was always very tempted with what Uncle Fingers offered him but there was just something about his uncle that made him nervous. Maybe it was his many prison sentences, maybe it was the facial tattoos, maybe the six mobile phones he carried around with him all the time, or maybe the way he was always looking over his shoulder and constantly wiping the end of his nose even though he did not have a cold; Timothy just did not feel he could trust the quality of his products, even though he did have some great bargains.

Despite this, in many ways, Uncle Fingers was the very best uncle you could wish for in times of trouble. Perhaps Timothy should take him up on that offer of using Muncher and Smasher as a way to put the bullies in their place?

Timothy decided that he would have to source a new product line himself and so he set his mind

Timothy & the Triplets Three

to it. However, with the fun of the Christmas performance, his rehearsals as the back end of the camel, the advent calendar, homework and re-watching all the old Christmas movies when they were on TV, he found it hard to focus.

He thought the best thing to do would be to leave it until the New Year when his mind would be clear. Maybe football memorabilia would be good ahead of the World Cup. But for now, he just wanted to enjoy Christmas.

Of course, the test tube triplet bullies were not planning on letting anybody enjoy Christmas, and so they made their own Christmas cheer (well, Neddy and Eddy did, anyway): forcing nice children to eat red hot chilli peppers, stealing tasty looking packed lunches, giving Timothy's friend a 'Santa stamp' on his toe and, of course,

Eddy's favourite torment of spraying water from his giant water pistol on boys' school trousers so it looked like they had wet themselves. Timothy sometimes had to spend an hour in the toilets trying to dry off his pants under the Flyson Hand Dryer.

After the Christmas performance of the Christmas Mashup, Mrs Giswellian needed to take a few days off. The rash on her neck refused to go away, she was shouting a lot and had been seen crying in the lunch hall surrounded by the caretaker team. The deputy headteacher tried to boost discipline in Mrs Giswellian's absence by raising his eyebrows at everybody. Timothy was not quite sure how this was supposed to instil discipline in a school of 1,800 children, but Mr Wollox was determined to try this approach.

Timothy & the Triplets Three

After a few days, Timothy and his friends realised that Mr Wollox was not raising his eyebrows in an attempt to boost discipline in the school. The fact was that Mr Wollox had developed a rather nasty twitch. So, Timothy and his friends decided it would be cruel to leave Mr Wollox struggling with this nasty twitch alone. In a show of solidarity, Timothy and his friends all decided to raise their eyebrows at everybody as well. They hoped Mr Wollox would appreciate their commitment to being part of his team.

Within hours, it became infectious, and there was rampant eyebrow raising everywhere. Mr Wollox would raise his eyebrows at the children, they would raise their eyebrows back, Mr Wollox would raise his eyebrows further, and the children would respond in a similar fashion. Eventually, everybody's eyebrows were on their foreheads.

Timothy & the Triplets Three

Some of the girls at school decided it was easier to draw their eyebrows on top of their foreheads, which Timothy had to admit looked quite good. Some of the boys decided to follow suit and draw eyebrows on the top of their foreheads. Soon, everybody joined in and the whole school had eyebrows drawn on top of their foreheads. The strange thing was, the more the children drew eyebrows on the top of their heads, the more Mr Wollox looked unwell.

Timothy & the Triplets Three

Within three days he had caught Mrs Giswellian's rash and was crying in the lunch hall with the caretaker team. He went off early for Christmas, just as Mrs Giswellian returned back to work. She held a special school assembly mass and said she was banning eyebrows drawn on foreheads. She thanked everybody for their solidarity with Mr Wollox but she felt the school should move forward without eyebrows raised.

Chapter 20
The last day of term

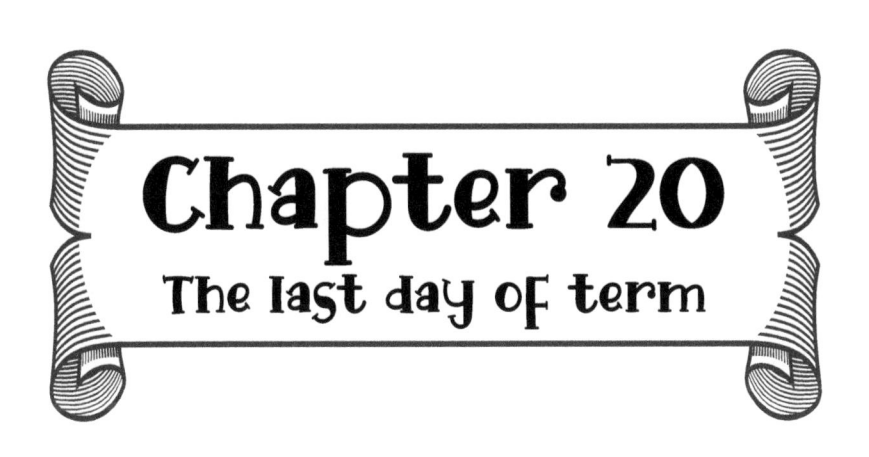

The final day of term arrived just days before Christmas and, as always, it was great fun. None of the teachers could be bothered to give the children proper lessons because the morning of the last day of term was when the teachers spent all of their time getting ready for the Christmas lunch. It was sort of like an own clothes day for the teaching staff. Even the male teachers changed their ties from stripes with a gravy stain to Rudolf the Reindeer with snowflakes.

Timothy & the Triplets Three

The art teacher wore jeans with a very large skull and cross bones badge on the belt buckle. One of the maths teachers wore leopard-skin high heel shoes for the first 15 minutes of the day before she replaced them with her comfy orange fluffy slippers which smelt of vomit. The caretaker always wore the same tight black silk shirt (with a button missing), which he left open from the waist up, revealing a forest of grey hair. On the back of his shirt was embroidered 'The USA West Coast 1951 Bowling Alley Team Champions', which Timothy thought was odd because when he asked the caretaker about it, he had told him he did not have a passport, he was born in 1972 and did not like bowling.

The female teachers wore skirts and dresses rather than trousers; this was often the only day of the year when it was possible to check if the female teachers had real legs. It would also explain why some of the female teachers' legs had whole forests growing on them. It would have taken a lot of wax to make those legs smooth and silky. Timothy made a mental note to remind himself to bring his camera the next year so he could take a photo of Mrs Whitehead's hairy legs for his dad. Mrs Whitehead won the prize for matching moustache and hairy legs for three years on the run. A couple of the teachers wore tinsel in their hair, a few put plastic antlers on their heads, and one wore a Santa mask, which was really strange and scared a few children because the white beard was not properly stuck on and so it was lopsided.

Timothy gave his friends chocolate selection boxes for Christmas. He had bought the selection

Timothy & the Triplets Three

boxes with the money he got from selling his old dartboard to a man in the next road. He had to find a way to raise money somehow after Neddy had stolen the money he had saved, so he placed an advert in the newspaper shop window to sell the dartboard. Although he really enjoyed playing darts with Dad, he wanted his friends at school to know how much he valued their friendship. It was ok though, because the next day the man brought the dartboard back. He didn't want a refund. He said that his wife was so very, very annoyed with him for buying a dartboard that he was just glad to get it out of the house and give it back to Timothy. The first time he had used it he had smashed the TV, nearly stabbed his mother-in-law, and the last dart had ended up in the ceiling. Apparently, his wife blew her top, so he thought it was best to get rid of it. He said he was going to buy a javelin for Christmas. This made Timothy's eyes open as wide as they ever had before; he just hoped the man's mother-in-law would be safe.

The selection boxes were very much appreciated by his friends, not least because they were still in date. He got lots of presents back: a colouring book (half completed), a radio with no batteries, a jigsaw with most of the pieces still in the box, and a lovely green woolly sock. (Timothy never found out where the other sock was, but he hoped it was having a great adventure wherever it was.)

The school canteen served a special Christmas lunch on the last day of term. For once, it was very special, not only because it was warm (rather than cold), but also because it tasted of a hint of

Timothy & the Triplets Three

turkey and the roast potatoes had been defrosted before they were served.

Mr Wollox was still off on special leave (he was having eyebrow lowering surgery), and Mrs Giswellian was coping – just about. No shouting this time but she still had a small rash on her neck. She had been told by her counsellor to count to three whenever she felt that she was about to start shouting. After a few days back in the headteacher's chair, she was regularly counting to 238 before the desire to shout passed.

It would have been much better organised if the school cook, Mrs McLurchen, had not put a case of brandy into the teachers' Christmas pudding. Some of the teachers smiled all afternoon, which was really out of character and worried a lot of the pupils. The last time the teachers had smiled that much was when they had bugged the room

Timothy & the Triplets Three

before the Fousted inspectors visited in school, so they could 'fix' the outstanding result.

Mrs Posh, the RE teacher, had a little too much to drink at lunchtime, as well as three helpings of the alcohol-laced Christmas pudding. Timothy knew she was a bit tipsy because she emerged from the staff toilets with her floral skirt tucked into her Christmas knickers. All the teachers and pupils agreed it would be too embarrassing to mention this predicament to her, so she spent all afternoon with her floral skirt tucked into her Christmas knickers – which matched her rosy cheeks very well.

On the last day of term, pupils were allowed to bring games to play in the afternoon – as long as they weren't too loud because the teachers always liked a nap after the lunch, especially Mrs Posh. Timothy took in 'Teachers vs Zombies 37'. In this version, the teachers all turned into zombies when your homework was late. You got points for putting the zombie teachers into the school duck pond. Timothy was particularly good at it and had the highest score for his class.

The test tube triplet bullies enjoyed the last days of school before Christmas because they managed to get away with even more mischief when the teachers' backs were turned. This year, they made a special effort to flick Christmas pudding flavoured

Timothy & the Triplets Three

chewing gum into classmates' hair. They told the younger children that Christmas was cancelled and stole the smaller children's mobile phones to send obnoxious texts to their parents.

Not all the big boys in school were bullies – there was Danny Steel. Danny was Timothy's hero. He was as tough as old boots and he wasn't scared of anyone. He never cried, he never worried, he was calm and laid back, yet no one messed with Danny. Timothy admired the fact that he was strong, carefree and bold, but he also knew that no one ever really knows how someone else is feeling inside because we are all so good at hiding our real feelings.

Danny had a way of looking at people which made them back away. He was one year older than Timothy and, although they didn't share

Timothy & the Triplets Three

any lessons or friendship groups, Timothy still admired him and considered Danny a hero. Danny had stuck up for Timothy a few times when the bully triplets were making his soul turn grey and miserable. Danny stuck up for everybody. He had been born without one of his feet, but he had a fantastic Road Runner Wheelchair with a 750cc electric motor, and an iPad attached to the handlebars. Danny never raised his voice, but he had this way of making his presence felt. Having one foot fewer than most people did not seem to bother Danny; he never felt sorry for himself. Timothy loved the way his wheelchair would sometimes connect with a bully's shins with a fantastic thud and a big smile from Danny. All the bullies in school learnt very quickly that their shins could not argue with a Road Runner Wheelchair with a 750cc electric motor.

Timothy & the Triplets Three

The last day at school was an opportunity for Danny to decorate his wheelchair as Santa's sleigh. He would wrap miles of tinsel around the frame. His dad made wooden panels which attached to both sides with a sleigh painted on, and his mum and nan made four huge fluffy reindeers to bolt onto the front. His big brother fitted a massive speaker to the rear so Danny could play Christmas carols all day. He also had a microphone so he could make special Christmas cheer announcements randomly throughout the day. "Ho Ho Ho, All Homework Is Cancelled Next Year!"

One of Timothy's favourites was:

"Jingle Bells, Jingle Bells, Jingle all the way,
Oh what fun it is to be in school on the last day."

Timothy & the Triplets Three

Father Mike popped into school to wish everybody a Merry Christmas. After three helpings of the teachers' Christmas pudding he decided to try out his latest songs: 'Shake it Off' and 'Rockstar'. He seemed to forget it was Christmas Eve the next day, but at least during his final encore he managed to invite everybody to his next 'concert' the following day – 'Rock Around the Crib'.

As father Mike sang, he shared a shower of dandruff which settled all around him like a layer of freshly laid snow. It was almost a beautiful Christmas card scene. It would have covered anyone who got to close, but luckily Father Mike was well known for his extreme bad breath, so everybody kept a safe distance anyway.

Some of the teachers just swayed gently as Father Mike sang, some of the teachers fell over, but most teachers slept noisily in the staff room.

Timothy & the Triplets Three

Mr Burke (Head of Sports) lived for this time of year when he could be in charge of the whole school on this one afternoon. The children nicknamed him Shout-a-lot because no one took any notice of him so he would shout all the time. It wasn't angry shouting but rather it was a happy type of shouting, almost as though he felt by shouting, he was earning the respect of the children. Nothing could be further from the truth, as many of the children wore headphones during Shout-a-lot's lessons so they could not hear a single word he said. He wore a very tight tracksuit to show off his muscle definition and six pack. However, it was so tight it actually showed off his love for beer and full English breakfasts.

It was tradition that, on the last day of school before Christmas, the sports department would organise a game of 'Hunt for Santa' for the

Timothy & the Triplets Three

afternoon's activities. Shout-a-lot would come in very early and hide 60 fluffy Santas around school, one for each form. The idea of the game was that you had to run around school trying to find the Santa for your form.

It was great fun. Children slid down banisters and locked each other in store cupboards. Tony Meaningless was only discovered on the 3rd of January last year, having been locked in the kitchen store cupboard for the whole of Christmas. But it was ok because no one had noticed at home and he quite enjoyed eating uncooked pasta, although he did have to wear dark sunglasses for a couple of weeks when he came out until he got used to seeing daylight again after the darkness of the store cupboard. On other years, some children kidnapped sleeping teachers in the staff room – which, on reflection, was not much fun because they were so fast asleep they never noticed they had been kidnapped. One smart group of 6th form students would hunt down the teachers who they suspected of having romantic feelings for each other. The goal was to wait until the couple thought they were alone and then burst in with the camera. These pictures were very valuable and had secured many lazy students an A* in their end of year exams.

Shout-a-lot would run around and exhaust himself blowing his whistle and trying to keep score. As the afternoon wore on, more and more children would just set off for home. By the time school ended, Shout-a-lot was usually left singing carols with the prefects.

Timothy was racing through the music room, enjoying himself in all the chaos, when he noticed Bert sitting on a chair on his own in the corner. His brothers were elsewhere setting off every fire alarm in the building. Taking a closer look, Timothy saw that Bert was not just on his own, he looked deflated, and was staring at his feet. Timothy didn't want to get any closer in case it was a trap, so he tiptoed out of the room to continue in his hunt for the Santas.

As he walked home, covered in tinsel, he wondered why Bert was not joining in the triplets' normal campaign of terror. Maybe Bert was taking a day off, he thought. Maybe bullies have to take a day off every now and then.

Chapter 21
The Growing Christmas Gravy

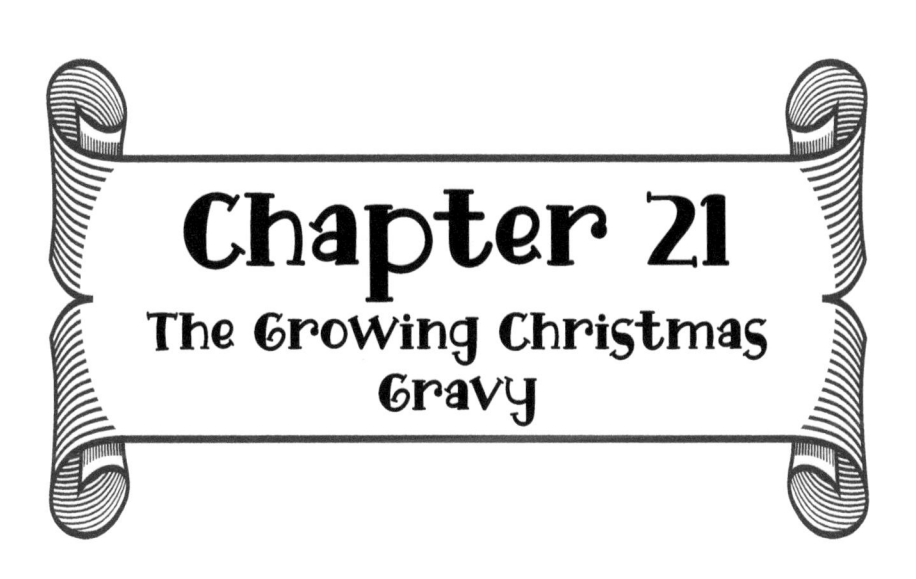

Christmas Eve started early in Timothy's house. At 4.30am Dad was dispatched to queue outside Sparks and Mencer so that he could be sure to get his order of turkey gravy. Mum was a great cook but there were problems with the gravy the previous year.

Mum had been really busy all morning – cooking, cleaning, baking, ironing – all in preparation for 'the locusts' (this was Dad's

Timothy & the Triplets Three

nickname for his wife's wider family who came for lunch on Christmas Eve… well, not all of them, just a couple, and Timothy knew who they were) to arrive. So, in the final moments of preparation, she asked Lulabella to stir the gravy whilst she jumped in the shower. Timothy was always baffled when his mum would say she was going to jump in the shower. In all his years living with his mum, he had never seen her jump in the shower.

Lulabella stirred the gravy as she sent text messages to her friends. In fact, she stirred a little and sent lots of selfies. Then Lulabella noticed a nasty smell. She glanced down and shrieked as she saw a pan of burnt gravy. Quickly, she poured a glass of sparkling water into the gravy. Now it resembled burnt watery gravy with bubbles. It was so watery she needed to thicken it up, so she grabbed what she thought was the bag of plain flour. She poured the flour into the burnt watery gravy with bubbles and it became burnt lumpy gravy with lots of bubbles. She stirred like crazy. She didn't even have time to text her best friend, Squidge. However, as the minutes ticked by, getting closer to the time Mum jumped out of the shower and came downstairs and the locusts arrived, Lulabella noticed that the gravy appeared to be growing. It was halfway up the pan. Two minutes later, it was three quarters of the way up the pan, and within a further two minutes it was bubbling over the top of the pan. The gravy was growing and growing and growing. It was now flowing all over the cooker and onto the oak wood floor. Lulabella tried to pour half of it down the sink but it would not stop growing. With gravy everywhere, Mum bounced into the kitchen with a huge smile on her face and a set of illuminated reindeer antlers clipped to her head. Within seconds the smile was gone, replaced by a "What have you done?" squeal.

The whole pan had to be thrown away. The locusts arrived and watched whilst Lulabella and her mum cleaned the floors, cupboards and cooker. Unfortunately, the gravy set hard in the sink, blocking the plug hole, so all the dishes had to be cleaned in the bath after the meal. (The sink would not be repaired until the 5th January, so this was how they had to clean their dishes after every meal over the Christmas holiday.)

It was as Timothy's mum was bent over the bath, scrubbing the bits of burnt potatoes off the roasting dish, that Nan identified the culprit of the whole debacle. Dad had confessed to putting self-raising flour into the plain flour tin in the pre-Christmas 'Great Tidy Up'.

Timothy & the Triplets Three

Dad was not spoken to until the New Year and he was never allowed to 'tidy' the kitchen again. However, Dad seemed to take this very well. Timothy noticed a small glint in his eye when he was told this news.

After lunch on Christmas Eve each year, Timothy's family would head off for Hatton Park. Hatton Park was a big International Rust property, set in acres of parkland and home to Santa's reindeer. Each year, Timothy and Lulabella had a tradition of visiting the reindeer before they joined Father Christmas in delivering all the children's gifts around the world.

Everyone was in high spirits until they arrived at the car park, when Timothy's shoulders slumped as he knew what was coming. When you entered Hatton Park you still had to pay for car

Timothy & the Triplets Three

parking, even though his father had already paid for an annual pass to visit the house and gardens. As with every other year, Dad argued with the attendant. Mum tutted and Lulabella joined in by saying it was a disgrace, enjoying the drama. The attendant told Dad it was not his rules but, even if they were, he would have written them the same so to just pay up. Dad tutted because he hated silly little rules like that, ones that made people 'in charge' feel important. Mum gave Dad 'the look' but he ignored her as he had now got into his stride and started to explain to the car park attendant that just because he had a high vis jacket on it did not make him King Tutankhamun. The man in the high vis jacket said he did not care what Timothy's dad thought. Lulabella sat back in her seat and looked out of the window in the other direction because she feared her dad was losing the battle with the man in the high vis jacket and didn't want to be on the defeated side. After a few stern glares, Timothy's dad paid for the parking.

Watching the attendant get smaller and smaller in the rear-view mirror, Dad moaned that anybody who wears a high vis jacket suddenly thinks that they are right, that they are superior to everyone else and they refuse to listen to common sense. It was at this point that Mum reminded Dad that he sometimes wore a high vis jacket for work.

"Mmm, but that's different," Dad sniffed.

Mum raised her eyes to the skies and decided to say nothing (but Timothy heard her tut under her breath).

Timothy was puzzled because even when they had made such a fuss and had paid for parking,

Timothy & the Triplets Three

they didn't park the car because it was so cold. They just drove around slowly looking for the reindeer. Eventually, they spotted the reindeer with their huge antlers. Lulabella and Timothy leapt out of the car, followed swiftly by Dad, who grabbed a photo of them standing in front of the animals. Mum helped by shouting out of the car window for Dad to hurry up, then rolled the window up quickly and turned the heater up. Dad urged Lulabella and Timothy to go closer to the reindeer. But Lulabella squealed, thinking the reindeer were going to eat her, and Timothy laughed so much he cried.

Once the photo was taken, it was off to Mum's friend's house for hot chocolate and Christmas carols. Mum's friend was called Mrs Berry and she was lovely but shouted a lot because she was deaf. Mrs Berry loved Timothy's mum because she baked her cakes. In fact, Timothy's mum did not bake the cakes really, but bought them from Mr Yeastly. However, she always managed to forget to tell Mrs Berry this small detail when she delivered the baked goods, only nodding benevolently when Mrs Berry said, "Aren't you clever!"

Eventually, after Mrs Berry had shouted at everyone, and Timothy's family had helped Mrs Berry to get rid of some of the cake, and they had exchanged Christmas cards, Timothy and his family headed home.

They were exhausted and full of cake as they retired to bed, having left treats for Santa and the reindeer. Everyone had sweet dreams as they waited for the magic of Christmas day.

Timothy & the Triplets Three

At 5.43am, Timothy woke; he then woke his mum, she woke Dad and they all tried to wake Lulabella, who was having none of it.

"Leave me alone; I am tired. It's 5.43am! Are you mad? Go back to sleep!" she snorted at the top of her voice.

However, eventually the spirit of Christmas entered Lulabella and she got up. She did not open her eyes because she was too sleepy, but at least she did get up.

The day was perfect; Santa had left snowy footprints on the stairs and hall carpet. The mince pies had been eaten and the milk half drunk. Huge sacks were overflowing with gifts, and everything had been delivered, even the penguins. Dad went and picked up Nan (and remembered to put her in the car for once). Nan complained about everything but secretly loved the fact that there was so much to complain about. Mum had Christmas dinner ready by 9.15pm, which was a new record. Lulabella did a fashion show of her new clothes, shoes and handbags. Cousin Lucy popped in, giggled, showed everyone her glittering red nail varnish with mini snowmen on each nail, then left. Dad fell asleep in front of the TV – well, he fell asleep during opening the presents, during dinner, during anything, but especially the TV. Timothy loved the whole day.

Chapter 22
Turkey Trifle

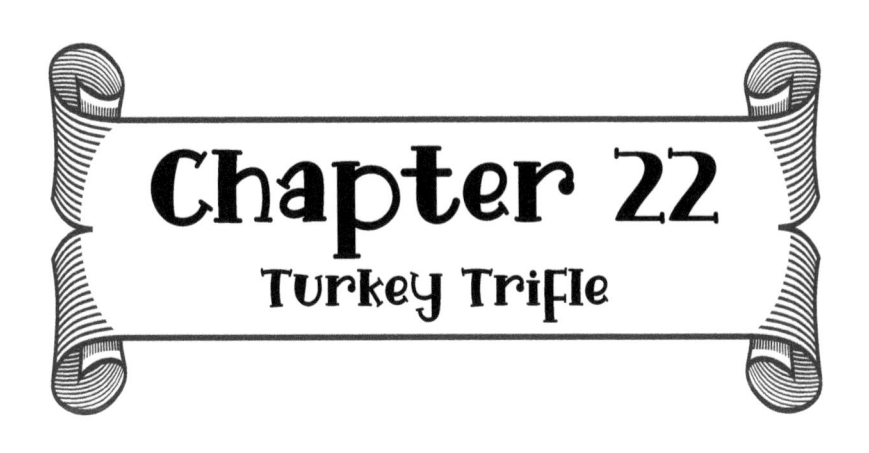

The next week was a blur. Every new toy and game had to be played with, batteries ran out and duplicate gifts were returned. Cash from cards was invested in even more gifts and the turkey was cooked in every way possible by Mum, including roasting, grilling, adding extra gravy, turkey curry, turkey sandwiches, turkey sweet and sour, turkey salad, turkey pie, turkey stew, turkey hotpot, turkey pasties, turkey cheesy slice, turkey with pineapple and coconut, turkey loaf, garlic and honey turkey risotto, turkey kebabs, turkey pizza, quiche with a hint of turkey, baked potato with turkey filling, turkey with chocolate sauce, turkey marzipan Christmas pudding (Lulabella's favourite), and finally, Timothy's mum's favourite, turkey trifle.

Cousin Lucy popped round for the family quizzes and board games. Lulabella spent days on her phone to her friends at university. Dad was in trouble for something most days. Mum cooked and cooked and cooked. Father Mike popped in, drank two bottles of sherry, blessed the Christmas tree, married cousin Lucy to herself and offered to christen a small teddy bear in the kitchen sink. Dad eventually took Father Mike home late in the evening, and he sat in the passenger seat singing 'I am lonesome tonight'.

Timothy & the Triplets Three

"I am lonesome tonight?

Did I bless you tonight?

I am sorry I just had to fart

Does your memory stray (like mine)?

To a bright sunny day

When I married you and called you sweetheart?"

Eventually there was no turkey left. The New Year was brought in and the Christmas tree taken down. The ugly truth was that Christmas was finished for another year. All that was left was the final Sunday, January 3rd – the last day before school started again on the Monday. Sunday, the 3rd was going to become a day Timothy would remember for the rest for his life.

Chapter 23
Crying over cakes

Sunday, the 3rd January started in a very ordinary way. Mum looked happy and smiled as she made breakfast. This was nothing unusual, Mum always looked happy and smiled. Dad looked happy and tried to smile. This was unusual because Dad was usually happy and always smiled. Watching Dad try to smile made Timothy nervous. Dad suggested that he and Timothy go out for a walk along the canal. This concerned Timothy because Dad was not slim and didn't like walking unless it was to a cake and coffee shop. Timothy knew there were no cake and coffee shops along the canal by their house, so he really was worried.

Timothy put his coat on and set out alongside Dad. As they walked along the canal Dad took hold of Timothy's hand and squeezed it tightly. They used to do this when Mum was telling Dad off for eating cakes, or being late, or not emptying the bin, making a mess, or telling naughty jokes, or going to bed late, or getting up late, or sneezing very loudly. So, in fact, you can see that Dad and Timothy held hands quite a bit. But this time, Dad was holding hands in a different way; it was almost as though he was looking for strength from Timothy. Dad then opened his mouth and explained that Nan did not have long to live and he should prepare himself for Nan not being in his life. Dad was a softie and often cried, but this was different. Timothy could tell he was devastated.

Silently, they walked home. Timothy knew the next few weeks would be strange, and he needed to be there for his mum and dad as Nan left this world and went to the 50p shop in the sky. 'What would happen when she arrived and did not like it?' he wondered.

Although life returned to normal in a way and Timothy went back to school, life was anything but normal. It was difficult for Timothy to deal with his Nan being ill and knowing that she would not be around for much longer.

Timothy's school friends would cluster around him and cover for him when he needed it most – usually in Maths or French, or when he wanted to get to the front of the dinner queue. Despite this, when Timothy first found out that his nan was dying, he felt so alone. None of his friends had ever been through this before. He thought no one would understand why he felt so sad and upset. He was angry; he would think over and over in his head, 'Why my nan? My nan never did anything wrong. My nan is lovely and wouldn't hurt a fly and she gets this awful illness. It's not fair!' Timothy knew this was not quite correct. His nan was often awful, she did not like anybody, and he suspected she had murdered several people at the bingo hall to improve her chances of winning the big cash prize. He was also convinced that she killed lots of flies and added them to her fruitcake mix.

Some days he felt so alone; he thought no one could possibly understand what he was going through. It was strange how it felt to watch his nan be unwell and he worried each time she went off to hospital. He didn't want to talk to people about it but he wished he had someone at school, his age, that understood how he felt. How could he be so alone when 1800 other children surrounded him at school? And yet, sometimes being surrounded by so many people makes you feel more alone. He didn't really want to talk about it; he just wanted it all to go away. He wanted his nan well again. He hated going home and watching Mum and Dad trying to be positive and happy. It was horrible.

Over the next few weeks, Nan got confused and called everybody the wrong names. She accused his mum and dad of locking her up in a prison. Timothy had to agree that the nursing

Timothy & the Triplets Three

home where they went to visit Nan was not very nice, but it wasn't a prison. Timothy's mum explained that there was something wrong with Nan's brain and this meant she was losing her memory. She explained it was not safe for Nan to live on her own anymore and that was why she had to live at Devilles Lodge. Timothy's nan kept asking him to get her out of the 'Devil's Lodge' when he went to visit.

"They keep me locked up and make me take drugs and only feed me once a day," she would whisper when his mum or dad left the room to speak to the care workers.

Timothy did not enjoy visiting Nan when she was like this, because it made him feel sad. So, for a couple of weeks Timothy was allowed to stay at his friends when his mum and dad went to see her – but then she got really ill.

Timothy & the Triplets Three

Timothy knew that Nan's health had become serious but he did not know why it was serious. Mum and Dad explained that Nan only had weeks to live and so it was important to visit her one last time.

On the day Timothy went to visit his nan for the last time, everybody at Devilles Lodge was very smiley. Everyone smiled at him and patted him on the back. It reminded him of when he won the egg and spoon race at school, but on the day of the visit there was no medal and no round of applause. Nan was asleep when they went into her room. She slept the whole time he was there and she was asleep when he left. Everybody smiled as he left. Mum and Dad took him for a crispy chicken mega meal at Captain Jack's on the way home as a treat.

Timothy & the Triplets Three

A few days later Nan was dead, and he was told she had gone to a better place. Timothy assumed it was like Devilles Lodge, but bigger. The doctor came and signed a death certificate to confirm Nan was dead. Timothy was confused. Nan had stopped breathing, she had stopped complaining, and she did not even want to go to the 50p shop. Everyone knew she was dead, so why did they need a doctor to sign a death certificate? Timothy suggested to his mum that it might have helped if the doctor had come the previous year and signed a certificate to prove she was alive.

The undertaker took Nan away in a black plastic bag and said they would look after her and bring her back to be cremated in a week. Father Mike visited and agreed to do the funeral

The next few days were filled with people calling at the house, bringing flowers (which

Timothy & the Triplets Three

Timothy thought was a bit odd because Nan was dead and wouldn't know about the flowers). People called at his house to drop off chicken soup, but also to ask if they could have Nan's fridge, chair, bed, wardrobe, lawnmower and big TV as she "wouldn't be needing them anymore". Timothy's dad didn't get annoyed with the requests from the 'vultures' (as he referred to them) and agreed to most requests, but he drew the line when a neighbour asked if he could have Nan's false teeth for his dog.

Most of the people who came to see Timothy's parents cried; some cried as they came into the house, some cried when they sat down and asked how they were coping now his nan had passed away, and some cried when they left – it was as though they were brave enough to hold the tears in until that final hug goodbye. Timothy wondered where the tears were stored before people cried. Perhaps it was in the bags under their eyes, or maybe in their bellies, and that's why older people have bigger bellies – so they can cry more.

Timothy wondered how much you had to cry before the tears ran out. He had cried for an hour when he had to cry for a competition. The lady next door cried for 10 minutes 14 seconds when she visited, until she had to leave because *Emma's Dale* had started (her favourite TV soap). Dad was difficult to monitor because he tended to have a little cry every time someone else cried. Timothy lost count so felt he should disqualify him from the contest. However, he decided to leave him in the competition because Dad did cry every day and showed no signs of stopping. Lulabella was brave and cried less but bit her lip more than anyone. Mrs Ritkiks wept and wept and wept. Timothy thought it might break a record, but once she found out that his nan's condition was not catching, she dried her eyes, finished her tea and cake, and left. Timothy concluded that she was actually crying about herself, so he disqualified her. Timothy's mum, however, did not cry, she smiled. She said she was not sad, Nan had lived a long and happy life and now she had gone to join Grandad. This was strange, because no one had mentioned Grandad since he left Nan for the tall, skinny lady in the fish and chip shop around the corner. Timothy wondered if Nan was going to meet him and the skinny lady from the fish and chip shop around the corner.

Despite her lack of tears, Timothy knew this was just his mum being brave, so in the end Dad won the crying competition and Mum won the bravery competition.

One of Timothy's jobs during the 'crying visitor' period was to make drinks and serve people cake. Timothy thought this was odd. His Nan has just died, yet everyone came over to the house for a hot drink and to eat cake. Dad was not happy. He kept trying to offer them digestive biscuits instead and then Mum would say, "Would you like some of our special cakes?" Dad even tried to say there were no cakes in the house when Uncle Fingers came, but Uncle Fingers went to investigate and found them in the cupboard shoved behind the 12 tins of tomato soup Dad kept for emergencies.

It wasn't just normal teas and coffees that Timothy had to make for the visitors. Cousin Lucy

Timothy & the Triplets Three

wanted peppermint tea whereas Father Mike wanted whiskey, but had to settle for a brandy latte. On one visit, Father Mike said he felt he should offer prayers for Timothy's nan. However, when he was looking for his prayer book in his bag, he found the music for 'The Wheels on the Bus' so he sang that instead. In many ways, it was much better than the prayers, because the sight of Father Mike singing 'The Wheels on the Bus' in the front room after several brandy lattes made everybody feel better.

In an effort to put people off visiting the house to cry and eat all the cakes, Dad started buying very strange cakes from Mr Yeastley. Ginger nettle and mint iced buns caused a stir, and pineapple inside-out cake with curry and chocolate was another one that tended to get left on the side of the plate. Dad would smile as Mum would glare at him. Timothy would chuckle; he liked it when Dad was naughty and Mum told him off. Dad getting told off by Mum felt normal and he desperately wanted everything to be normal.

Chapter 24
Going to the 50p shop in the sky

Eventually, the visits started to fade out. There was less of a need for tissues and the crying subsided. This was great, because there was more cake.

At the funeral, Father Mike sang 'Someone You Loved' beautifully. Everyone thought he may say a few prayers, but Father Mike said he did not want to drag the party down. Although he got Nan's name wrong, he did get her age right, which everyone thought was lovely.

Timothy & the Triplets Three

There weren't many people at the funeral. That was quite a surprise to Timothy because lots of people had turned up to the house to cry and eat cake. Thinking about it though, Nan had been horrid to lots of people for a long time. However, there were some of the lovely staff from the 50p shop who turned up because they said they would miss her complaining about everything.

The service at the crematorium was odd. Timothy stood silently, his eyes closed, hands in his pockets and a lump in his throat. Although he was sad, he was not that sad. In fact, he didn't know how he felt. He had half swallowed a Neverton mint just as they had arrived at the crematorium, so he sucked on that throughout the service.

Everyone waited for the sound of the rollers rolling his nan away. Moments earlier, the curtains had swept in front of her coffin and the only sound was a few weeping noises from his family to the accompaniment of Frank Sinatra crooning 'I Did It My Way' over the crematorium sound system. Eventually, Father Mike banged his tambourine and thanked everyone for coming Even though he was very jolly and full of positive words, he struggled to get the whole congregation to leave the crematorium conga style.

Timothy found it difficult to believe that Nan was dead. However, he knew she was dead because everyone had been talking about it for days. People were "sorry" she was dead, they were "shocked" she was dead, they "surprised" she was dead and a few people said it was "better" that she was dead.

He understood why people were shocked, surprised and sorry she was dead, but he had to ask his mum why it was better that she was dead. Mum explained that it was nothing to do with the fact that she was very grumpy, had smelly breath and green teeth, or that she rarely recognised anybody when they went to visit, but some people thought it was "better" to be dead than to be in pain and live the life she did at the end. Timothy was not unkind, but if the grounds for wishing people were dead was how grumpy they were, he could think of a few other candidates for the crematorium.

Even Uncle Fingers came to see Mum when Nan died. He wanted to know what Timothy's mum was going to do with all of Nan's old clothes and old wigs that she wouldn't need in that big 50p shop in the sky. Timothy asked what on earth would Uncle Fingers want with his Nan's old clothes, wigs and hats? Uncle Fingers explained he thought he could use them as part of his disguise wardrobe when "borrowing things from banks and building societies." Mum said she was very sorry, but they had a deep sentimental value and she could not dream of letting him wear them to do his jobs.

Uncle Fingers was not worried and smiled cheerfully as he said he was going to kidnap some garden gnomes later that day and expected a windfall for the ransom.

Chapter 25
Mrs Hen

Although Nan had died and been burnt to a cinder, the real problem was that the triplets, Eddy, Neddy and Bert, still made a real effort to make Timothy's life a misery. They would call him names, punch him, trip him up, hide his sports bag, push him in the mud, spit in his hair, spit in his food, say horrible things about his family, lie to get him in trouble and cheer when they made him cry.

In the past, Timothy had been able to cope with the triplets' nastiness because he only got the same as everyone else. The triplets were grotesque to everybody; they managed to make almost everyone cry at some point in the year – including the teachers. But since Nan's death, Timothy had found it more difficult to turn the other cheek. Eddy was there, leading the charge, followed closely by Neddy punching people in the face. Timothy knew it was all part of growing up. But now life had changed. Life was grotesque at home as well and so this just made it almost impossible to cope with the triplets.

When Timothy thought about it, he realised that Bert (who was still limping) just sort of followed the other two around, trying to smile and even occasionally saying sorry for his brothers' behaviour. However, his brothers seemed to be even worse than usual.

Timothy & the Triplets Three

One day, Timothy knew he would sort the triplets out once and for all. There was a part of him who wanted to let his alter ego, Ralph (the DVD debt collector), sort the triplets out, but he knew it would lead to too much trouble. His mum and dad had enough trouble at the moment without introducing Ralph to the situation.

Timothy hadn't wanted to go back to school after his Nan dying but, although he was not feeling 100%, his mum said he still had to go. The thought of having to face the triplets made everything worse. The night before he returned to school, he drew up a list of potential solutions to stop the bullying triplets making his life so miserable:

Timothy & the Triplets Three

1. ***Uncle Fingers*** – but that would lead to Uncle Fingers being back in prison and his mum would not be happy.
2. ***Lulabella*** – she would love the chance to be amazing but she was leaving for USA the next day.
3. ***Shark attack*** – no sharks in his neighbourhood.
4. ***Earthquake*** – it would hurt everyone, not just the bullies.
5. ***Kidnap*** – no one would ever pay a ransom, not even Mr and Mrs Fullofsnot.
6. ***Aliens*** – this had huge potential, but the aliens would not want to take them to their planet in another galaxy.
7. ***Bungee Jumping*** – the three bullies were scared of heights.

Timothy & the Triplets Three

He knew he was desperate when he looked at some of the ridiculous ideas. As if a shark would attack three Fullofsnots – they would taste awful.

There was nothing for it, he had to return to school. How on earth could he solve his agony?

Timothy had to tell everyone at school about Nan going to the big 50p shop in the sky – although most people seemed to already know, which made it a bit easier. Timothy just wanted everything to be normal and for nobody to mention his nan's demise, but there always seemed to be something or someone that would remind him of her. One day it was the nice young drama teacher, Miss Smith, who would smile and pat him on the shoulder in a way that showed she cared. Another day they discussed dying in science, and that was tough.

Timothy & the Triplets Three

Mrs Giswellian organised a mentor to see Timothy every week to check he was ok. Mrs Hen (his school trauma, family break-up, bereavement and unhappiness counsellor) was really kind; she was really, really kind. She had weepy puppy dog eyes and always nodded at everything you said. She carried a box of tissues everywhere she went and she called Timothy 'deary', even though he kept reminding her that his name was Timothy. She would just nod and tell him, "I know, I know, deary, the pain just has to flow out of you." Timothy would say he was fine, but Mrs Hen was not going to give in so easily. She had recently completed a Japanese counselling course which highlighted the positive effect that living on raw onion for six weeks can have on your general levels of happiness. Therefore, she was always offering tearful teenagers a raw onion. She would say, "I know it doesn't taste great, but it will make you happier once it has stopped making your eyes water." Timothy wondered how on earth Mrs Hen could tell whether someone was crying because they were unhappy or if their eyes were just watering because of the raw onion.

One day, Mrs Hen asked, "Is there anything you want to share with me, Timothy?" After a long pause, he admitted there was something and took out of his pocket half a bag of sour jelly frogs he had bought the day before. She smiled and said, "Deary, deary me, my little lemon-flavoured lovie, what a sweet angel you are. Can you tell me where you are hurting?" Timothy told her about his in-growing toenail – the one Eddy, had stamped on just before Christmas – which had green and yellow puss coming out of it. At that point, her digital watch alarm went off to remind her she needed to visit another poor soul who was in pain. "Deary, don't try to be too brave, I am always here if you need me." Timothy thought this was strange because it was not true. He had asked her to get him out of his French exam the next week and she had said no. He asked her to do his maths homework the previous night and she said no. He had asked her to sponsor him to raise money for Africa the next month and she said no. So, actually, she was only there for him when it suited her (2.30pm on a Tuesday) and when she did not have another pressing case of a teenager in distress.

Sometimes when Timothy was on his way home, he would see Mrs Giswellian and Mrs

Timothy & the Triplets Three

Hen crying together in the headteacher's office when it had all become too much for them. This actually cheered him up no end.

One of the other things that cheered Timothy up was the fact that the bully triplets had become the bully twins. Bert did not seem to be around as much, and Timothy hoped he had been expelled or moved to another school. He would try to remember to ask Father Mike to pray for this result at Mass on Sunday.

Some of the teachers were great, they just were great. You couldn't describe why but you just knew they really cared rather than pretending to care. When you passed a 'great' teacher in the corridor at school, they would smile and wink, or just put their hand on their heart and smile at him. This meant so much.

Timothy & the Triplets Three

The drama teacher, Miss Curtain, took him to one side at the end of one of her lessons (they had been learning how to be a tree in a storm) and said, "I sense you don't really want to talk about your Nan passing away." Timothy had nodded. "Ok, I can understand that. I care about you and I am sorry your nan has died, but I don't want to intrude or be nosey. You know I am always here for you when you just want to sit quietly and not have to say anything." Timothy nodded again. "So my idea is whenever I see you around school, I will just put my thumb out to you and waggle it up and down. All I want you to do is to show me your thumb and put it up if you are having a good day, put it down if it's a bad day and you want some time, or put it in the middle if things are okish and you are ok on your own."

Timothy & the Triplets Three

Timothy smiled and put his thumb up. Miss Curtain smiled and put her thumb up too.

Chapter 26
Best Friends

Of course, his friends did what they could to look after him, but none of them had had the same experience so couldn't possibly understand what Timothy was going through. However, his classmates managed to help him sometimes forget about the sadness of losing his nan.

In his form he had the usual collection of 12-year-old boys and girls, many who were fun to be around. Alistair (or Spewy as he was known to his friends) used to spew up everywhere until they found out he was allergic to eggs. Spewy's mum was from Delhi and his dad was from Birmingham. This meant he was able to speak Hundu and Birminghamese languages. Spewy did not mind being sick and so he was quite happy to be sick to order. Other children in the class would save their egg and cress sandwiches and feed them to Spewy in the French exam or during chemistry practical. This would result in Spewy being sick over the egg donor who was then sent home. Rumours suggested that Spewy would often get requests to throw up over a teacher who wanted the afternoon off. Spewy would happily oblige and throw up over the teacher. His best trick was sucking blue raspberry sherbet sweets then swallowing raw eggs. This meant he was able to spew frothy blue puke out of his nose like a fountain. Timothy and his friends always gave him a huge round of applause when he was able to pull off this trick.

Billy was fun and lived an amazing life because he told everyone his dad was Spiderman. No one had ever met his dad, so it was hard to verify if his dad was Spiderman or not. Someone said his dad was in jail for house burglary and his nickname was Spiderman because he always broke into the house by climbing up the walls. However, Timothy thought it was more fun to believe Billy's dad was the real Spiderman as Uncle Fingers had never mentioned him and he was in jail all the time so was bound to have seen him if he had been there.

Julie was tall and the netball captain. She was able to unscrew the lights in the classroom ceilings without a ladder. She didn't remove the lights, but unscrewed them just enough so they

Timothy & the Triplets Three

didn't work. It was great fun when the teachers would stand for hours switching the lights on and off before complaining to the caretaker. Also, Julie had the longest hairs under her arms of anybody in Timothy's year.

Lionel was short, spotty and top of maths. He smelt of roses and garlic. When Lionel smiled broadly he was able to burst some of his spots on command, squeezing puss out of the ripest ones. Sometimes the puss would just dribble down his chin, but sometimes he could aim it at people who were stood alongside him. Mr Wollox was a direct hit one day, and everybody cheered. Lionel just kept smiling as more and more torpedoes of puss left his face, covering the teacher.

Simon was quiet. Everyone knew him as the bogey eater for obvious reasons. Jane was plain and always wore odd socks. Hilda was an awful girl; she was loud, often angry, and wore the most horrific fringe with great pride. Timothy wondered if she had such a bad temper because she had secretly pushed a nail through her tummy button because she could not afford to get it pierced. Hilda's only redeeming feature was she was the daughter of a prison officer. This was really helpful when Timothy needed to get a message to Uncle Fingers in a hurry.

There was a red-haired girl call Jillie who was covered in freckles; you could hardly see her nose because of the freckles. She was the school chess champion. Timothy wanted to use her at one of the Christmas fairs. Instead of the usual 'Guess the Weight of the Cake' competition, he wanted Jillie to walk around the school with a sign on her saying 'Guess how many freckles are on my face'. Jillie refused. She was from Scotland. This was

Timothy & the Triplets Three

tough for her because no one could understand a word she said.

Timothy had been to Scotland once with his dad. They went on the train to Glasgow. During the journey, he was wondering what it would be like in a country where all the men wore kilts and everybody ate haggis. Timothy had never seen a haggis. He had goggled haggis farms and not found one. He had tried to find a breeder of haggis, but none were to be found. Maybe they were more commonly kept as a pet. Perhaps there was the equivalent of Crufts for haggis.

When the train stopped at Glasgow Central Station, he had been surprised. None of the men wore kilts and he couldn't see a single haggis shop anywhere in sight. If that wasn't a big enough shock, Timothy was amazed that everybody he met spoke with a Scottish accent. At first he thought it was a trick and that everyone was pretending to have a Scottish accent. But as he watched closely, they were even talking to each other in a Scottish accent. Timothy's dad explained that Scottish people are very proud of their accent and spend a lot of time at home practising speaking Scottish. Timothy thought this was odd. The more they practised, the harder it was to understand anything they said. Timothy would say, "Hello, it's very nice to meet you." The Scottish people would reply, "Ach, goooonna be a greeeeeet deeeee." Timothy decided the best thing to do was to smile politely, nodding like Mrs Cluck-Cluck did at school.

On this trip he also learnt that lots of Scottish people wanted to separate Scotland from the rest of the United Kingdom. As they travelled back

Timothy & the Triplets Three

home on the train, Timothy slept and dreamt about all the JCB diggers it would take to separate Scotland from the rest of the UK. Where would they take Scotland once it was separated? Maybe they wanted to attach it to America like the 53rd state, glue it next to New York. Or maybe they wanted to float it out to Africa to get better weather? Well, he thought it was shame because it seemed to him to be a perfect fit exactly where it was, but Timothy was only 12 years old and he still had a lot to learn.

The other class bully was Jimbo; he was football captain and had huge ears. That's why he was called Jimbo to his face and Jumbo behind his back. However, sometimes he would hear people call him Jumbo because he had excellent hearing. He loved punching smaller children.

Timothy & the Triplets Three

The trouble was that Jimbo's ears were so big that when you saw him you just could not take your eyes off his ears. You ended up talking to his ears and not his face. When he talked, his ears would move, and when he sang in assembly, his ears would jiggle in time with the music. It was great to watch, but it did make you giggle. On hot days, children would try to sit behind him in the dining hall. When Jimbo ate his lunch, his wiggling ears would create a lovely draft that was very welcome on a hot, sweaty summer's day.

Timothy managed to measure Jimbo's ears once when he fell asleep in RE. They stuck out from his head 10.2 cm! Now that's really big. You may not think 10.2 cm is very big, but that was for each ear. So, across the whole of his head, it was 22.4 cm. When you compare this against the biggest nose in the school – which was only 7.9

Timothy & the Triplets Three

cm and belonged to Mrs Butcher, the dinner lady – you have to give credit where it is due, Jimbo had a massive pair of ears. Timothy wanted to enter him in the Big Book of Records, but when he rang them, no one believed that there was a boy in his class with such huge ears.

One day, Jimbo punched Lionel because he thought he called him Jumbo. This was a big mistake. Lionel turned around, pushed both of Jimbo's arms out of the way, punched him on the end of his nose and kicked his knee, bending it the wrong way. Everyone was shocked; Lionel was a short, spotty maths champion, covered in puss, but quiet and never hurt a fly. What they didn't know was he was also a Ju-Jitsu black belt. Jimbo clearly did not know this either. Everyone was also shocked because Jimbo went down and did not get up. His leg was twisted in a really strange way. The teacher called for first aid, the first aid called for an ambulance, and the ambulance called for a helicopter which took Jimbo to hospital. He didn't return to school for six weeks. When he did come back, his ears were just as big but he never punched anybody again. Lionel was suspended for a week, but when he came back to school he was considered to be a short, spotty maths champion and school hero (and Ju-Jitsu Master).

The history teacher moved Timothy to sit next to Lionel when he returned to school. Timothy asked the history teacher why he had been moved. She said it was not his position in life to ask a teacher why she did things, it was the teacher's position in life to ask him questions, so that was that. So, Timothy sat next to Lionel in history class and did not ask the history teacher any more questions. This was hard though, because when the history teacher's teaching was really awful and Timothy could not make any sense of anything she said, he knew he could not ask her any questions so he just sat there and wondered how many times a giraffe blinked in an hour.

One day, right in the middle of Henry the VIII beheading one of his wives, Lionel nudged Timothy and put his thumb up, then put his thumb down, then put his thumb in the middle. Timothy opened his eyes wide. He blinked and watched whilst Lionel repeated the process. Timothy smiled, put his thumb up and he knew they were going to be friends for life.

Over the next few weeks, Timothy got to know Lionel better and found out that his grandad had died just before Christmas. It felt great to have one friend who understood. Sometimes they would go and see Miss Curtain together and sit and say nothing for 10 minutes, but it really helped.

Lionel and Timothy would become good friends over the next few years. Lionel even taught Timothy Ju-Jitsu and took him to the Ju-Jitsu club. Best of all, they trusted each other and knew they could tell each other anything and it would never be shared. That meant a lot to Timothy, and to Lionel as well.

Chapter 27
The Fullofsnots Visit

When Timothy arrived home from school one day a few weeks into the school term, his mum was on the phone and she seemed upset. He wondered if Cousin Lucy was dating Stevo again or if Uncle Fingers was back in prison for a short stay. Perhaps Father Mike had finally gone to Graceland in the sky?

When she came off the phone, she explained that bully triplet Bert was in hospital and very poorly. She said that his limp over the last few

Timothy & the Triplets Three

months was nothing to do with Stevo knocking him over, but he had a rare condition that was very serious. Mrs Fullofsnot had rung Timothy's mum to see if she would put an appeal for a bone marrow donor in the PTA and church magazines. Timothy's mum had agreed to do just that and was typing an appeal as she told Timothy the story.

Timothy had mixed feelings about what his mother was telling him because a part of him was sad for Bert, but a part of him was pleased because it would stop him from making Timothy's life a misery. He was confused and so he just fell silent and went up to his bedroom to spend some time on his own.

He knew his mum would want to help Mrs Fullofsnot because she was lovely and helped everyone, but it also made him angry. Deep down,

Timothy & the Triplets Three

he did not want his mum helping Bert, the bully triplet monster.

Timothy had never told his mum, dad or sister about the way the triplets bullied him because he felt embarrassed and ashamed of the way they abused him. Somewhere inside, he believed it was his fault that he was bullied, and he did not want to worry Mum and Dad about it. He did not tell Lulabella because she would go around to their house and sort them out. This would have been great until she went back to USA and he would be left alone with them again, so he just kept quiet and told no-one.

Well, there was only one other person Timothy told about the triplets (apart from Uncle Fingers) and that was Uncle Tony. Uncle Tony was Timothy's dad's brother. Some people said Uncle

Timothy & the Triplets Three

Tony was different to other people – and he was.

He had a partner called George and that made him different, but it's not what Timothy meant when he said he was different. Uncle Tony was different because he treated him like an adult, smiled a lot and always asked him if they could chat and have a catch up. He had warm eyes and a kind heart. Without fail, he dressed smart and always looked like he had just stepped off a catwalk and smelt like a film star. (Actually, Timothy didn't know what a film star smelt like but Uncle Tony smelt the way he imagined a film star to smell).

Sometimes Uncle Tony would call and ask Timothy is he wanted to go with him for a walk. Sometimes he would just phone up and, after speaking to Dad, he would ask to speak to Timothy for a quick catch up.

Timothy & the Triplets Three

He always bought Timothy great Christmas and birthday presents which had lots of thought in them. He had great music in his car. Although he was two years older than Timothy's dad, it was as though he was twenty years younger.

Uncle Tony was cool and Timothy trusted him. When Timothy told him about the bullies, Uncle Tony listened and nodded. He didn't make any big suggestions or run to school to blab to the teachers, he just quietly sat and listened.

At the end of the latest update on the triplets, Uncle Tony had said, "Look Timothy, just remember you are strong and they are weak. Be strong. Lots of people love you because you are Timothy. When the bullies stand in front of you, just think of that love and how strong you are." He told Timothy that anybody who finds joy in ridiculing and beating up young children for their own enjoyment has many deep-rooted problems.

Although it didn't change anything, it actually changed everything. Timothy was strong and he knew he was loved. Uncle Tony was always there when he needed him.

The last time they chatted on one of their walks, Uncle Tony asked how Bert was because he had seen the local TV reports of his need to find a bone marrow donor quickly as he was very unwell. Timothy could feel his face go red, and when Uncle Tony asked why he was embarrassed, he said it was because when he had heard that Bert was unwell there was a part of him that was glad. Timothy could feel himself getting upset because although he had felt glad to begin with, he felt awful and very guilty soon after. Uncle Tony did not judge Timothy, he just said

Timothy & the Triplets Three

he thought it was a natural response after the sadness Bert and his brothers had caused him. The good thing was that Timothy had reflected on his reaction and had realised that this wasn't how he wanted to live his life. Now he had the chance to resolve it. Uncle Tony said the bravest person is the one who offers their hand in friendship to someone who has caused them pain.

School was a little less horrifying over the next few weeks. Eddy and Neddy were really quiet and had not been so nasty. They even stopped punching people. News of Bert was not good. Apparently, he was really ill and Father Mike was by his bedside serenading him day and night with Elvis' Greatest Hits. Timothy suspected this may have been why he wasn't feeling so good.

Timothy & the Triplets Three

For once, Mum had not been able to pull off a miracle and find a bone marrow donor for Bert. Timothy felt good about this, but then awful that he felt good, so in the end he felt awful. Life was very confusing.

Chapter 28
Dad makes a donation

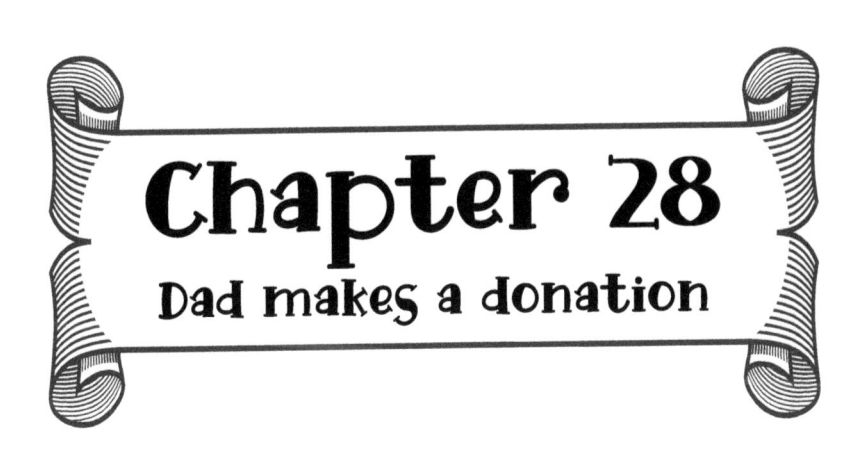

Timothy's mum had not given up and was organising a 24-hour disco to raise money in case Bert Fullofsnot had to be flown to USA to get treatment. Mum wanted Timothy to play the music. He tried to explain how horrid Bert had been to him over the last few years but she insisted. No one ever said no to Timothy's mum, including Timothy.

However, other events overtook the 24-hour disco planning. Timothy's dad came home early

Timothy & the Triplets Three

one day and had a long chat in the front room with mum with the door closed. Timothy's mum and dad never closed the door on the front room, so he knew it must be serious. Maybe Dad had been promoted and they were going to live in Australia. Maybe Dad was getting a new car. Maybe Dad had lost his job or maybe Dad was doing a sponsored sky dive covered in blue custard to raise money for Bert Fullofsnot. Eventually the door opened and they invited Timothy to come in and sit down.

Timothy's dad explained that the company where he worked had encouraged all the staff to fill in an organ donor card. His dad explained that he hadn't wanted to fill one in (and he had never got round to filling it in at Lent either), but everybody was doing it, so he felt daft saying he was scared. The hospital had contacted Timothy's

Timothy & the Triplets Three

dad to go in for some tests. The tests were done the day before and had confirmed that he was an ideal bone marrow donor for Bert Fullofsnot.

Timothy was in shock and couldn't say a word. He did not want his dad to be a donor for Bert Fullofsnot. Bert had made his life a living misery for years. Timothy was angry and worried about his dad. It didn't help when Timothy's mum said it was a good thing and it needed to happen quickly to save Bert's life. This made Timothy even more confused and angry. Bert had made his life unbearable, but he did not want Bert to die.

Dad said Mr and Mrs Fullofsnot were coming around later that night to discuss the situation. Timothy didn't know what to say so he went to sit on his own in his bedroom. He worried about everything, feeling confused, angry, hurt and upset. How could his dad want to help one of the

Timothy & the Triplets Three

three bully boy triplets who had caused him so much pain? But what if his dad didn't help Bert? What would happen then? The Fullofsnot triplet bullies had hurt him so much for so many years and now they were going to hurt his dad and make him unwell. When would they be satisfied? Would they ever give up? Did Bert really need a bone marrow transplant or was it just a trick? He dismissed that last thought. He knew Bert had been unwell for the last few months, and he was sorry about that. Bert was the least awful of the triplets and it would be awful if he died. Why couldn't somebody else be a donor? Surely there was someone living far away who could be flown half-way around the world to save Bert. Why did it have to be his dad who was the donor? Why couldn't Eddy and Neddy donate their bone marrow? Or his parents? He wondered if

Timothy & the Triplets Three

Bert's own parents had refused to donate their bone marrow. He knew that if the boot was on the other foot, Bert would not donate his bone marrow to save Timothy's dad, so why should he help them? The Fullofsnots never helped anybody. They never donated to any of Mum's raffles, so why should Dad have to help them now?

At about 7, Timothy heard the front doorbell ring, the door open and his mum and dad talking quietly downstairs. Eventually, after about an hour, he heard his mum's soft footsteps on the stairs. She put her head around the door and asked him to come down to meet the Fullofsnots and to hear about the plan. Very reluctantly, he went downstairs, and to a massive surprise – Eddy and Neddy were sat in his front room.

Timothy & the Triplets Three

Mrs Fullofsnot explained that when she went to school she had been bullied by a group of girls who excluded her from everything. She was always on her own, and they never spoke to her in the class or at break times. These girls drew nasty pictures of her, told lies about her and tripped her up on the way home from school. They stole her bag and put it down the toilet. As a result, her time at school was very sad. As she got older, she was very shy and so when Mr Fullofsnot showed romantic interest in her she was so happy, because being 6 foot 6 inches tall, she knew he would be able to protect her from bullies for the rest of her life.

She said that she and her husband had always tried to be good parents and so when Bert became ill they were very worried. The doctors explained he was very weak and the outlook was grim unless they found a donor. That was why she had approached Timothy's mum to publish an appeal for a donor in the PTA and church magazines. She knew Timothy's mum was lovely and hoped she could help. When it turned out Timothy's dad could be a donor they were thrilled. However, this turned to horror for her when Eddy and Neddy had to come clean about their awful bullying of Timothy and other children at school.

Timothy & the Triplets Three

Mrs Fullofsnot then broke down in tears, saying she felt she had totally failed as a mum. How had her children end up as bullies when her own childhood was ruined by bullies? The last thing she wanted was for other children to suffer the way she had suffered at the hands of bullies, and yet here were her own three sons who had turned out to be the worst of the worst. She explained that she loved them but she was ashamed of their behaviour. She had even researched to see if the reason they were bullies was because they were made in a test tubes, but the doctors had assured her this was just a coincidence.

As she was crying and telling Timothy the story, Neddy and Eddy sat with their heads down, not saying a word.

Mr Fullofsnot comforted his wife and said that he loved his sons, but he was also ashamed of their behaviour. As a 6 foot 6 inch teenager, people assume you don't get bullied, but actually you do get picked on because everybody needs to prove they can punch the biggest boy in school. He had never been able to get the school bus home because the bullies at his school would take the opportunity to target him. So he had always walked home on his own and became very lonely. For many years, he had no friends and became a loner.

He was also ashamed to admit that he had sometimes bullied other smaller children and older people like Mr Yeastly. He did not like this part of his character and had worked hard to become a better person.

He got a job as a painter and decorator because he could work on his own (and, of course, he could paint the ceilings without a ladder, which was

Timothy & the Triplets Three

very helpful). So, when he met Mrs Fullofsnot, he immediately fell in love because she was the first person who showed him any kindness. These two broken souls had come together to be strong. Mr Fullofsnot admitted he had found it very hard to learn that his test tube triplets had terrorised hundreds of children. He looked at his sons as he said this, but neither of them raised their heads. In fact, Timothy thought he saw a tear drop from Neddy's face to the carpet.

After a pause, Mr Fullofsnot explained that, in recompense, the family had agreed to set up a charity and raise money to tackle bullying.

He said, "We know a lot about bullying as a family. We have been in touch with a counsellor and we are all signed up to work through our bullying problems. Isn't that right, boys?" Neddy and Eddy finally raised their heads and nodded, but immediately dropped them again to stare at the carpet.

"We can then roll this help out to children everywhere. The charity will be called 'The Fullofsnots Bulling Helpline Thanks to Timothy's dad'."

Mrs Fullofsnot added that it would be known as TFBHTTTD for short.

There was a silence as everyone took this information in. Mr and Mrs Fullofsnot then said their two sons had something they would like to say. Eddy and Neddy stood up, their faces red from crying, and said that they knew they had spent the last six years bullying Timothy. They knew that they had repeatedly upset him and made his life a misery. Eddy apologised for his awful behaviour and Neddy even said sorry for punching him so much and so hard. Taking it in turns, they explained that going to visit Bert had made them realise how bad they had been to others. They were really worried about Bert because he was so ill. As they shuffled their feet, they said they understood that their apology did not make everything alright and Timothy's dad had every right to refuse to be a bone marrow donor. However, they just wanted to say a huge sorry. Eddy said that they had been really stupid and wanted to try to put it right. The last eight weeks had been very difficult for the Fullofsnot family and it made them realise how wrong it had been to behave so badly to so many people.

At this point, they had to stop for a bit as they were both trying very hard not to start crying again. Their father put a hand on each of his sons' shoulders in support and this gave them the strength to continue.

Timothy & the Triplets Three

Eddy and Neddy said that they had never known that both their parents had been bullied and that it had made them so sad when this had been explained to them. They could not justify why they had become such awful bullies but they hoped the counselling would help them understand it all. Neddy said that when they were young and first come to school, Father Mike had led a school assembly about how wonderful it was that they were made in a test tube. Ever since then, the other children had teased them about being made in a test tube. They got teased that much that they would cry at the end of every day. So, in the end they discovered that the only way to stop other children teasing them about being made in a test tube was to hit them really hard. Neddy said the problem was that once you start hitting people, it seemed the only way you could earn respect and get attention. So they just starting hitting everybody to get maximum attention and respect.

Neddy shrugged his shoulders and said he wanted to find a way to stop doing it. Timothy was stunned and trying his best to take it all in. He had no idea what to say. Eddy then walked over to Timothy, said sorry and offered to shake Timothy's hand. Neddy followed suit.

Although Timothy accepted the handshake, he was confused. He knew he had joked about them being made in test tubes and giggled behind their backs with his dad. Did that make him a bully?

Timothy looked around the room: Mr and Mrs Fullofsnot were holding each other very tightly; Neddy and Eddy had slumped shoulders and were obviously full of remorse and seeking forgiveness; and Timothy's mum was holding hands with his dad and biting her bottom lip.

Timothy & the Triplets Three

The silence was broken when Timothy's dad walked up to him, put Timothy's hand in his hand and said, "Timothy, we are all so sorry about what you have been going through all these years. We have let you down. We should have known something was happening so that we could give you more support. But we didn't and you have suffered. We are all so sorry. Now we have the chance to do something positive to heal all this upset and save Bert." Mrs Fullofsnot let out a small wail at this point. "But we have all agreed tonight that you can make the final decision over whether or not I agree to be a donor to save Bert." Mrs Fullofsnot let out another louder wail. "If you are comfortable with it, I will be a donor, but if you don't feel comfortable, I will not do it. You are in control, Timothy."

Mrs Fullofsnot was now sniffing loudly into her hanky.

Timothy & the Triplets Three

"What would you like me to do, Timothy?" Timothy's dad asked.

The whole room fell silent, apart from Mrs Fullofsnot snuffling into her hanky whilst holding her husband's hand.

Timothy thought long and hard then said that of course he was still wounded by the behaviour of the triplets, but working together to save Bert was much more important.

The Fullofsnots cheered and hugged everyone. Dad cried because of Timothy's bravery. They agreed to meet the doctors at the hospital the next day.

Timothy rang Uncle Tony and told him his news. Uncle Tony said he was even more proud of him because he had forgiven the Fullofsnots. Who would have thought that he, Timothy, would save the day?

Chapter 29
The end of CRABz

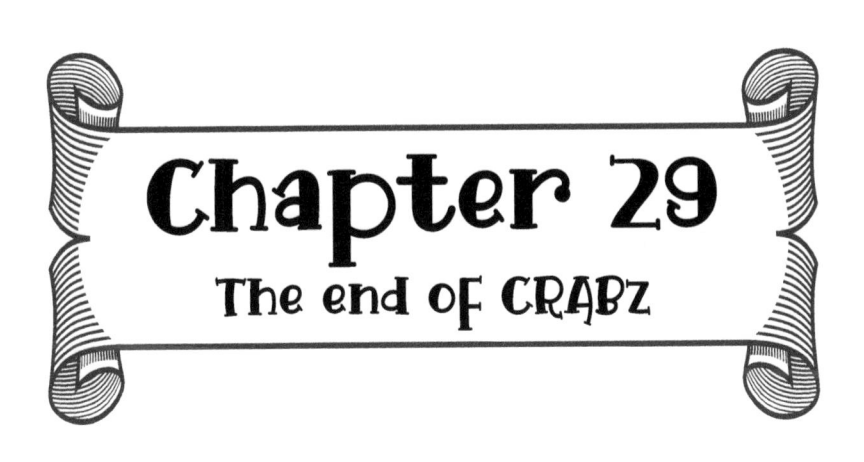

After that, Eddy and Neddy were reformed characters. They formally disbanded the CRABz crew and were positive and good fun with everyone. Uncle Fingers organised a party to celebrate the end of CRABz, and the ex CRABz members retrained to become ballet dancers, knitting experts and worm collectors. Eddy and Neddy followed Timothy everywhere, every day, like a pair of Hollywood bodyguards.

Timothy & the Triplets Three

Timothy's dad donated the bone marrow one week later. Timothy, Lulabella and Mum went to see him every day in hospital and Timothy was so proud. He had always been Timothy's hero, but this kindness elevated him to a new high.

Timothy also went to see Bert every day. He was very unwell before the operation and even immediately after it, but he got stronger with each passing day. Bert and Timothy became good friends; they did homework together, and they played 'Gut Wrench Ice Hockey Version 24' on Timothy's portable Today Station.

Mr and Mrs Fullofsnot were very grateful and bought a full-length Jaws 24 DVD for Timothy and his family. Mr Yeastly baked enough cakes to feed the whole hospital. Father Mike praised Elvis for his divine intervention and made him an instant super hero.

Timothy & the Triplets Three

Timothy would like to report that they all lived happily ever after, but they did not. Some days are good, but on other days, sad things happen.

Eventually, Father Mike passed on to that big stage in the sky. Father Pavel returned from the M25 and took over Mass full time.

Mr Shout-a-lot got louder and eventually exploded all over the sports hall just before half term.

Timothy's dad made a full recovery and his mum is still raising money to save other souls.

Hilda's temper got worse, then she met a lovely boy called Geraldo who would sing her love songs, send her notes with love hearts on, bake her chocolate cookies, hold her hand, give her bunches of flowers and write her endless poems about how her eyes reminded him of twinkling stars. Hilda fell madly in love and floated around school for months until she found out Geraldo was baking lots of cookies for other girls who had eyes like twinkling stars. So then Hilda went back to losing her temper again.

Mrs Ritkiks bought another cat which had kittens. They didn't like Lemon Meringue Pie either, but ate it to please Mrs Ritkiks.

Mrs Giswellian believed that she had given birth to kittens and made herself a nest in the storeroom, so she was encouraged to leave school – she become a female body builder – and Mr Wollox was appointed the new headteacher. Spewy cheered everybody up by spewing on the new headteacher on his first day.

Mr Fullofsnot decorated Timothy's house, with the help of Eddy and Neddy, and became good friends with Timothy's dad. They discovered that they both had the same warped sense of

Timothy & the Triplets Three

humour. Timothy, Spewy, Jillie, Billy, Father Pavel, Mr and Mrs Fullofsnot, Simon, Mrs Butcher, Mr Himalaya, Cousin Lucy, Stevo and even Mr Yeastly and his cookery friend Prince Humphrey of Denmark are in training to swim the channel in the summer to raise money for a cat sanctuary

Timothy's mum wants to create a charity with Mrs Ritkiks for lost and abandoned cats. When Timothy's mum tried to include Lulabella, she just laughed and said, "I rather think not."

Timothy learnt that bad things happen sometimes, but only you can sort them out, and you can do anything if you set your mind to it. He also learnt that it was important to talk to other people about the bad things that happen.

Timothy & the Triplets Three

The TFBHTTTD has grown and grown into a global charity. Timothy's mum and Mrs Fullofsnot run it together, and it helps children and adults everywhere who suffer from bullying or have become bullies and don't know how to stop bullying. The TFBHTTTD has produced golden rules for children who are being bullied:

- Write down how you are feeling and keep a record of each bullying incident.
- Find an adult you can talk to and share your feelings. This may be a parent, family member, teacher, doctor, policeman or youth worker, somebody you can trust.
- As upsetting as these events are, don't forget you are not alone and there are solutions which can help.

Timothy & the Triplets Three

- Support anyone you think is being bullied.
- Report any behaviour you see of a child being bullied to an adult.
- Find a buddy who you can talk to and get support from when you are being bullied.

So, if you are reading this story and you are being bullied, or a friend of yours is being bullied, I know you will have bad days and feel very alone. Reach out, find someone you can trust, talk your feelings over, and together you will be able to find solutions.

Many of us have been bullied and we all find our own way to happiness – you will too.

Resources

Resources to use if you need help due to bullying;

https://www.nationalbullyinghelpline.co.uk

https://youngminds.org.uk/find-help/feelings-and-symptoms/bullying/

https://www.nspcc.org.uk/what-is-child-abuse/types-of-abuse/bullying-and-cyberbullying/

https://www.anti-bullyingalliance.org.uk/tools-information/if-youre-being-bullied/find-help-and-support

https://www.kidscape.org.uk

https://www.bullying.co.uk

https://www.childline.org.uk/info-advice/bullying-abuse-safety/types-bullying/

https://www.supportline.org.uk/problems/bullying-at-school/

https://bulliesout.com

https://www.bbc.co.uk/programmes/articles/5Ffpz77jVbLvjsFj9GvKd8l/information-and-support-bullying